a good word
for a great day!

365 DAILY INSPIRATIONS

A Good Word for a Great Day!
365 Daily Inspirations

Copyright© 2013 by Inprov, Ltd.
ISBN 978-0-9833462-5-8
For further information, write Inprov, at:
2150 E Continental Blvd, Southlake, TX 76092

Scripture quotations marked (NIV) are taken from THE HOLY BIBLE, NEW INTERNATIONAL VERSION®, NIV® Copyright © 1973, 1978, 1984, 2011 by Biblica, Inc.™ Used by permission. All rights reserved worldwide.

Scripture quotations marked (NLT) are taken from the Holy Bible, New Living Translation, copyright © 1996, 2004, 2007 by Tyndale House Foundation. Used by permission of Tyndale House Publishers, Inc., Carol Stream, Illinois 60188. All rights reserved.

Scripture quotations marked (NKJV) are taken from the New King James Version®. Copyright © 1982 by Thomas Nelson, Inc. Used by permission. All rights reserved.

Scripture quotations marked The Message are taken from The Message. Copyright © 1993, 1994, 1995, 1996, 2000, 2001, 2002. Used by permission of NavPress Publishing Group.

Scripture quotations marked (Phillips) are taken from the J. B. Phillips, "The New Testament in Modern English", 1962 edition, published by HarperCollins.

Scripture quotations marked (NCV) are taken from the New Century Version®. Copyright © 2005 by Thomas Nelson, Inc. Used by permission. All rights reserved.

Scripture quotations marked (AMP) are taken from the Amplified® Bible, Copyright © 1954, 1958, 1962, 1964, 1965, 1987 by The Lockman Foundation. Used by permission.

Scripture quotations marked (KNOX) are taken from The Holy Bible—Knox Version. © Westminster Diocese

Scripture quotations marked (NASB) are taken from the New American Standard Bible®, Copyright © 1960, 1962, 1963, 1968, 1971, 1972, 1973, 1975, 1977, 1995 by The Lockman Foundation. Used by permission.

Scripture quotations marked (NLV) are taken from The Holy Bible – New Life Version. © Christian Literature International

Scripture quotations marked (NET) are taken from the NET Bible® copyright ©1996-2006 by Biblical Studies Press, L.L.C. http://netbible.com All rights reserved.

Scripture quotations marked (HCSB) are taken from the Holman Christian Standard Bible®, Copyright © 1999, 2000, 2002, 2003, 2009 by Holman Bible Publishers. Used by permission Holman Christian Standard Bible®, Holman CSB®, and HCSB® are federally registered trademarks of Holman Bible Publishers.

Scripture quotations marked (GW) are taken from GOD'S WORD®, © 1995 God's Word to the Nations. Used by permission of Baker Publishing Group.

january

1

above

Then my head will be exalted **above** the enemies who surround me; at his sacred tent I will sacrifice with shouts of joy;
I will sing and make music to the LORD.

Psalm 27:6 (NIV)

. . . .

You are fully equipped to rise **above** every obstacle you face,
big or small. God is on your side and He has not left you alone.
Rejoice in knowing that victory is yours today!

absolute

How great is our Lord! His power is **absolute**! His understanding is beyond comprehension!

Psalm 147:5 (NLT)

· ·

Today, you can rest in knowing that God is in control. He is sovereign, faithful to His promises and His power is **absolute**! There is nothing in life that He has not already overcome on your behalf.

january

abundant

You haven't done this before. Ask, using my name, and you will receive, and you will have **abundant** joy.

John 16:24 (NLT)

. . . .

The Lord longs to bless you. Ask Him to pour out His abundant joy, peace, goodness, patience, rest, provision and favor into your life. He promises to give all that you need and more. He is **abundant** life!

january

accepted

Accept one another, then, just as Christ accepted you, in order to bring praise to God.

Romans 15:7 (NIV)

. . . .

You are completely **accepted**. You are fearfully and wonderfully made. Today, walk in confidence knowing that God loves you, and choose to love others with the same love that Christ has shown you.

accomplished

LORD, you establish peace for us; all we have **accomplished** you have done for us.

Isaiah 26:12 (NIV)

. . . .

The Lord has done great things! On the cross, Jesus conquered death. And through Him, you can reign in life. Take hold of the peace that is yours and boast in His **accomplishments**.

january

6

achieve

. . . So is my word that goes out from my mouth: It will not return to me empty, but will accomplish what I desire and **achieve** the purpose for which I sent it.

Isaiah 55:11 (NIV)

. . . .

The Word of God is living and active. Speak His Word into your circumstances and watch Him move on your behalf. God will **achieve** His purposes in your life when you align your words and actions with His Word.

january

7

acknowledge

"Whoever acknowledges me before others, I will also **acknowledge** before my Father in heaven."

Matthew 10:32 (NIV)

A life in pursuit of Jesus is the greatest purpose any person can serve. Christ died to make you perfect in the eyes of the Father. What a privilege to **acknowledge** such a Savior before men!

acquire

To **acquire** wisdom is to love oneself; people who cherish understanding will prosper.

Proverbs 19:8 (NLT)

. . . .

Wisdom **acquired** from God is far greater than any wisdom man can offer. God wants to fill you with wisdom and understanding that will produce great fruit in your life and bring true and lasting success.

january

9

active

Declare me innocent, O LORD, for I have **acted** with integrity;
I have trusted in the LORD without wavering.

Psalm 26:1 (NLT)

Trust in the Lord today and know that He is the defender of
the weak. Rest in the goodness of the Lord. He will **act** on
your behalf.

january

10

adapt

Do nothing that might make men stumble, whether they are Jews or Greeks or members of the Church of God. I myself try to **adapt** myself to all men without considering my own advantage but their advantage, that if possible they may be saved.

1 Corinthians 10:32–33 (Phillips)

. . . .

God has called us to love others with His love. We can demonstrate His love by **adapting** our ways and methods. Remember, what might be acceptable to you could cause another to sin. God wants to love others through you!

january

11

admiration

"Watch out! Don't do your good deeds publicly, to be **admired** by others, for you will lose the reward from your Father in heaven."

Matthew 6:1 (NLT)

. . . .

Let your good works be motivated by God's love. The **admiration** of others is gratifying, but it is the Lord's "Well done" that represents the greatest reward. Seek the approval of Him and He will pour favor into your life.

january

12

adoration

Yours, O LORD, is the greatness, the power, the glory, the victory, and the majesty. Everything in the heavens and on earth is yours, O LORD, and this is your kingdom. We **adore** you as the one who is over all things.

1 Chronicles 29:11 (NLT)

· ·

Praising the Lord will bring life to your spirit. He is the creator of all things, victor over darkness and His name is to be praised. Live in **adoration** of Him, for He adores you!

january

13

affection

Set your **affection** on things above, not on things on the earth.

Colossians 3:2 (KJV)

. . . .

The things of this world are temporary. Focus your eyes on Jesus, and He will never disappoint you. Before you were born, your heavenly Father set His **affections** on you.

january

14

always

Your statutes are **always** righteous; give me understanding that I may live.

Psalm 119:144 (NIV)

. . . .

The ways of the Lord are flawless. His plans never fail. He is **always** faithful, always righteous and always good!

amazing

How **amazing** are the deeds of the LORD! All who delight in him should ponder them.

Psalm 111:2 (NLT)

. . . .

The Lord wants to do **amazing** things in your life and through your life. If you need a miracle, He is the God of the impossible. Stand and believe in the goodness of your Father!

january

16

ambition

How should you learn to believe, you who are content to receive honour from one another, and are not **ambitious** for the honour which comes from him, who alone is God?

John 5:44 (KNOX)

. . . .

Be **ambitious** for the things of God. Seek honor from the Lord and not from man. His reward is eternal, but reward from man fades away.

amiable

How **amiable** are thy tabernacles, O LORD of hosts!

Psalm 84:1 (KJV)

. . . .

The presence of the Lord is inviting, full of love and grace. His beauty is like nothing you have ever seen. His ways are **amiable** and peaceful!

january

18

anchored

Evil people try to drag me into sin, but I am firmly **anchored** to your instructions.

Psalm 119:61 (NLT)

. . . .

Sin is no obstacle when you are **anchored** to God's Word. His Word is all the power you need to break free of any distractions or temptations you'll face today.

armed

You have **armed** me with strength for the battle; you have subdued my enemies under my feet.

2 Samuel 22:40 (NLT)

. . . .

One of God's promises is that we are victorious over our enemies. He has **armed** you with every weapon you need to fight and win! As the Bible asks, "If God is for us, who can be against us?"

january

20

arrival

Not that I have already obtained all this, or have already **arrived** at my goal, but I press on to take hold of that for which Christ Jesus took hold of me.

Philippians 3:12 (NIV)

. . . .

You have not **arrived** at your fullest potential! The Lord wants to take you further and higher than you could possibly dream.

january

21

aspiration

The **aspirations** of good people end in celebration; the ambitions of bad people crash.

Proverbs 10:28 (The Message)

. . . .

Your heavenly Father works all things for your good. **Aspire** to be like Him and then He will bring your dreams to pass. Trust Him and then He will make your path straight.

attainment

Gray hair is a crown of splendor; it is **attained** in the way of righteousness.

Proverbs 16:31 (NIV)

. . . .

The righteousness of God is a gift to you; it is not something you must **attain** by your own works. Jesus died so that you are righteous in the Father's eyes. Rest and accept His righteousness today!

january

23

attraction

And I, if and when I am lifted up from the earth [on the cross], will draw and **attract** all men [Gentiles as well as Jews] to Myself.

John 12:32 (AMP)

. . . .

Jesus told His followers that people would know His disciples by their love. In the same way, God's unconditional love will **attract** others to you. Ask the Lord to continually fill you with His love for others!

january

24

authenticity

For if the message given through angels [the Law spoken by them to Moses] was **authentic** and proved sure, and every violation and disobedience received an appropriate (just and adequate) penalty, how shall we escape [appropriate retribution] if we neglect and refuse to pay attention to such a great salvation [as is now offered to us, letting it drift past us forever]?

Hebrews 2:2–3 (AMP)

. . . .

Authenticity is rare in the world today. Be real with those people around you so they might be drawn to the truth and life found in Jesus Christ!

january

25

awaken

Because I am righteous, I will see you. When I **awake**, I will see you face to face and be satisfied.

Psalm 17:15 (NLT)

. . . .

Awake each morning with a high level of expectancy in the Lord. He wants to work and move in extraordinary ways on your behalf!

january

26

awesome

They shall speak of the might of your **awesome** deeds, and I will declare your greatness.

Psalm 145:6 (ESV)

. . . .

As you go about your day, praise the Lord for the **awesome** things He has done in your life. Thank Him for the things He has yet to do! The Lord is great and worthy to be praised!

balance

A just **balance** and scales belong to the LORD; All the weights of the bag are His concern.

Proverbs 16:11 (NASB)

. . . .

Do not worry about the judgments of men; the Lord holds the **balance** of right and wrong. Walk in integrity and God will be your Peacemaker.

january

28

beauty

He has made everything **beautiful** in its time. He has also set eternity in the human heart; yet no one can fathom what God has done from beginning to end.

Ecclesiastes 3:11 (NIV)

. . . .

True **beauty** is found within a person; it is not defined by the outward appearance. Remember, man looks at the outward appearance, but the Lord looks at the heart.

january

29

believe

"If you **believe**, you will receive whatever you ask for in prayer."

Matthew 21:22 (NIV)

Your heavenly Father longs to give you the desires of your heart. Make your requests known to Him. **Believe** in His faithfulness and He will answer you.

beloved

Beloved, let us love one another, for love is from God, and whoever loves has been born of God and knows God.

1 John 4:7 (ESV)

. . . .

You are God's **beloved**. He loves you with a love that is unconditional, unfailing and perfect. God is love, and He wants to love others through you.

january

31

beneficial

"I have the right to do anything," you say—but not everything is **beneficial**. "I have the right to do anything"—but I will not be mastered by anything.

1 Corinthians 6:12 (NIV)

. . . .

What is good for someone else might not be **beneficial** to you. God has a unique calling and plan for your life and He has the very best in store. Don't settle for second best!

benevolence

Let the husband render unto the wife due **benevolence**, and likewise also the wife unto the husband.

1 Corinthians 7:3 (KJV)

. . . .

Benevolent is the Lord! As an excellent husband is faithful and good towards his wife, so is the Lord towards His people.

february

2

best

This is what the LORD says—your Redeemer, the Holy One of
Israel: "I am the LORD your God, who teaches you what is **best**
for you, who directs you in the way you should go."

Isaiah 48:17 (NIV)

. . . .

Your heavenly Father has bigger dreams for you than you have
for yourself. When God says "no," it is because He has something
far better planned. Don't settle for less than God's **best**!

february

better

Because your love is **better** than life, my lips will glorify you.

Psalm 63:3 (NIV)

. . . .

God's love is captivating and fulfilling. God's love is limitless and eternal. God's love is real and pure. God's love is even **better** than life!

february

4

beyond

God's voice thunders in marvelous ways; he does great things **beyond** our understanding.

Job 37:5 (NIV)

. . . .

No matter the depth of our knowledge in this world, the greatness of God goes far **beyond** our understanding. Seek wisdom and learn His ways, but most of all, draw near to His heart!

february

big

I have not hidden what is right and good with You in my heart. I have spoken about how faithful You are and about Your saving power. I have not hidden Your loving-kindness and Your truth from the **big** meeting.

Psalm 40:10 (NLV)

. . . .

The Lord's plans for you are **big**! Do not listen to those who say you are not talented or gifted enough. God is mighty in you!

february

blameless

He holds success in store for the upright, he is a shield to those whose walk is **blameless** . . .

Proverbs 2:7 (NIV)

. . . .

Because of Jesus Christ, you are **blameless** in the eyes of the Father. He no longer sees the sin and everything that once separated you from Him. He sees His Son in your place. You are righteous through Christ!

february

7

blessed

Blessed are those who find wisdom, those who gain understanding . . .

Proverbs 3:13 (NIV)

. . . .

True wisdom and understanding can only come from God; and He longs to give it to you. The Bible says God gives wisdom freely to those who desire it. You are **blessed**!

february

8

bloom

Our days on earth are like grass; like wildflowers, we **bloom** and die.

Psalm 103:15 (NLT)

. . . .

Time passes quickly, just as flowers **bloom** and die. Cherish your days on this earth. There is a time and a purpose for everything!

february

9

boundless

Although I am less than the least of all the Lord's people, this grace was given me: to preach to the Gentiles the **boundless** riches of Christ . . .

Ephesians 3:8 (NIV)

. . . .

Because you know Jesus as Savior, you have more than this world could ever offer. God's grace, provision, favor, goodness and freedom in your life are **boundless**!

february

brightly

The light of the righteous shines **brightly**, but the lamp of the wicked is snuffed out.

Proverbs 13:9 (NIV)

. . . .

Christ has freely given you His righteousness by faith. You are a **bright** light in a world that desperately needs Jesus. Shine your light into the darkness!

february

11

brilliance

His coming is as **brilliant** as the sunrise. Rays of light flash from his hands, where his awesome power is hidden . . .

Habakkuk 3:4 (NLT)

· ·

The splendor of the Lord is beyond imagination. He holds all power within His hands. The **brilliance** of God is too great for human eyes!

february

12

brotherly

Love one another with **brotherly** affection. Outdo one another in showing honor.

Romans 12:10 (ESV)

. . . .

When you prefer others over yourself, you will be amazed at the blessings God pours into your life. Just as Jesus laid down His life for mankind, love others out of that same **brotherly** love as children of God.

called

Therefore do not be ashamed of the testimony of our Lord, nor of me His prisoner, but share with me in the sufferings for the gospel according to the power of God, who has saved us and **called** us with a holy calling, not according to our works, but according to His own purpose and grace which was given to us in Christ Jesus before time began . . .

2 Timothy 1:8–9 (NKJV)

You are **called**. You have been given a future and a hope. The God of the universe created you for a specific purpose, and He will complete it!

february

14

calm

Fools give full vent to their rage, but the wise bring **calm** in the end.

Proverbs 29:11 (NIV)

. . . .

In the midst of trouble, do not give way to anger. Remember, there is wisdom in remaining **calm**, and there you will find peace.

february

15

capable

Who can find a virtuous and **capable** wife? She is more precious than rubies.

Proverbs 31:10 (NLT)

. . . .

You are **capable** of great things! Today, be confident in the gifts and talents God has given you. He has not called you to anything He has not already gifted you to accomplish!

february

16

care

Come, let us bow down in worship, let us kneel before the Lord our Maker; for he is our God and we are the people of his pasture, the flock under his **care**.

Psalm 95:6–7 (NIV)

. . . .

Your heavenly Father **cares** for you! He is your Protector and Defender just as a shepherd watches over his flock of sheep. Rest in His provision.

february

change

"I am God and always will be. No one is able to take anything out of My hand. I do something, and who can **change** it?"

Isaiah 43:13 (NLV)

. . . .

The Bible says if God is for us, no enemy can stand against us. God has everything under His control, and there is no power and no enemy that can **change** what His hands have touched!

february

18

charity

But when you do a **charitable** deed, do not let your left hand know what your right hand is doing, that your charitable deed may be in secret; and your Father who sees in secret will Himself reward you openly.

Matthew 6:3–4 (NKJV)

. . . .

A reward from the Father is far greater than any reward from man. Your **charitable** works do not go unnoticed. Do them for the glory of God, not the glory of man. Your reward is great!

february

19

chastening

Chasten your son while there is hope, And do not set your heart on his destruction.

Proverbs 19:18 (NKJV)

. . . .

In the moment, discipline is painful and hard, but in the end it protects from a greater consequence—maybe even destruct-ion. Your Father **chastens** you because He loves you and wants you to succeed!

february

20

cheerful

A happy heart makes the face **cheerful**, but heartache crushes the spirit.

Proverbs 15:13 (NIV)

. . . .

Today, may the Lord give you a happy heart and a **cheerful** face! May His joy overwhelm you and His presence be your delight!

february

21

cherished

If I had **cherished** sin in my heart, the Lord would not have listened; but God has surely listened and has heard my prayer.

Psalm 66:18–19 (NIV)

. . . .

The Lord listens to the heart that yearns for Him and His righteousness. He **cherishes** all who draw near to Him. Draw near to Him and He will draw near to you!

february

22

childish

Dear brothers and sisters, don't be **childish** in your understanding of these things. Be innocent as babies when it comes
to evil, but be mature in understanding matters of this kind.

1 Corinthians 14:20 (NLT)

. . . .

Ask the Lord for understanding and desire the things of God.
Put away your **childish** ways of thinking. True maturity is found
in the Lord.

clean

"The voice spoke from heaven a second time, 'Do not call anything impure that God has made **clean**.'"

Acts 11:9 (NIV)

. . . .

What the Lord calls pure is pure and what He has made **clean** is clean. Jesus qualified you for righteousness not according to your works or the things of this life; it is according to His great love.

february

24

clearly

Clearly no one who relies on the law is justified before God, because "the righteous will live by faith."

Galatians 3:11 (NIV)

. . . .

The law demands of you, but God's abundant grace supplies to you. The Lord has made it **clear** that our righteousness is not from the works of our own hands, it is a gift from God, the gift of Jesus!

february

25

cleverness

For Christ didn't send me to baptize, but to preach the Good News—and not with **clever** speech, for fear that the cross of Christ would lose its power.

1 Corinthians 1:17 (NLT)

. . . .

The enemy will use clever words and do whatever it takes to keep the lost from hearing the good news of Christ. But **clever** speech is not necessary when spreading the gospel because the cross of Christ speaks for itself. God's Word is all the power we need!

closeness

Watch your life and doctrine **closely**. Persevere in them, because if you do, you will save both yourself and your hearers.

1 Timothy 4:16 (NIV)

. . . .

Diligently seek the Lord and His truth. Walk **closely** with Him and He will direct your steps to save you from the enemy.

february

27

comfort

Even though I walk through the darkest valley, I will fear no evil, for you are with me; your rod and your staff, they **comfort** me.

Psalm 23:4 (NIV)

. . . .

The Lord is with you in the midst of trouble and He knows your heartache. Let Him be all the **comfort** that you long for and the light that leads you out of the darkness.

february

28

commitment

He always stands by his covenant—the **commitment** he made to a thousand generations.

Psalm 105:8 (NLT)

. . . .

The promises of God stand forever; He is fully **committed** to you. The allegiance of man is temporary, but the faithfulness of the Lord never fails!

march

1

companionship

Run from anything that stimulates youthful lusts. Instead, pursue righteous living, faithfulness, love, and peace. Enjoy the **companionship** of those who call on the Lord with pure hearts.

2 Timothy 2:22 (NLT)

. . . .

True friends are a gift from the Lord. Your **companions** shape your character. Travel the road of life with those who long to be like Jesus and pursue His heart.

march

2

compassion

The LORD is gracious and righteous; our God is full of **compassion**.

Psalm 116:5 (NIV)

. . . .

God is full of **compassion** and His heart aches deeply for the lost and hurting. If you are brokenhearted today, know that the Lord wants to heal and restore your brokenness and replace it with His joy and life through Him.

march

complete

No one has ever seen God; but if we love one another, God lives in us and His love is made **complete** in us.

1 John 4:12 (NIV)

. . . .

Even though no one has ever seen God, we know Him because of His great love for us. When He resides in our hearts, His love is made **complete** as He loves others through us. God is love!

march

4

confidence

. . . being **confident** of this, that he who began a good work in you will carry it on to completion until the day of Christ Jesus.

Philippians 1:6 (NIV)

· ·

Be **confident** in the Lord's plans for your life. He has promised to complete the work that He began, and all you have to do is trust in His goodness!

considerate

But the wisdom that comes from heaven is first of all pure; then peace-loving, **considerate**, submissive, full of mercy and good fruit, impartial and sincere.

James 3:17 (NIV)

. . . .

Long for understanding and seek wisdom from God. The wisdom of God will bring peace, purity, **consideration** of others, favor, mercy and sincerity to your life.

march

6

consumed

His disciples remembered that it is written: "Zeal for your house
will **consume** me."

John 2:17 (NIV)

. . . .

Today and every day, your heavenly Father wants to **consume**
you with His goodness, grace, favor, blessing and presence.
Open up your heart to ALL of Him!

march

7

control

For the love of Christ **controls** us, because we have concluded this: that one has died for all, therefore all have died . . .

2 Corinthians 5:14 (ESV)

. . . .

Your heavenly Father wants complete **control** of your life. You can let go of every burden and lay it at the feet of Jesus. Your Father longs for you to walk in peace and rest.

march

8

convinced

For I am **convinced** that neither death nor life, neither angels nor demons, neither the present nor the future, nor any powers, neither height nor depth, nor anything else in all creation, will be able to separate us from the love of God that is in Christ Jesus our Lord.

Romans 8:38–39 (NIV)

. . . .

Are you **convinced** of the Father's great love for you? His love is far beyond the love that any man could hope to give. His love is captivating, unfailing and altogether beautiful!

march

9

correction

Preach the word; be prepared in season and out of season; **correct**, rebuke and encourage—with great patience and careful instruction.

2 Timothy 4:2 (NIV)

. . . .

The Lord's **correction** is for your good. His desire is to keep you from trouble and destruction. Wisdom, success, favor and encouragement are found within His Word.

march

courage

"Be strong and **courageous**. Do not be afraid or terrified because of them, for the LORD your God goes with you; he will never leave you nor forsake you."

Deuteronomy 31:6 (NIV)

. . . .

You are victorious over the enemy! Be **courageous**, for God who lives within you is greater than he who is in this world.

march

11

crafted

But God made the earth by his might; he shaped the world by his wisdom, **crafted** the skies by his knowledge.

Jeremiah 10:12 (CEB)

. . . .

Every detail of your being was **crafted** by the Creator of the universe. From the hairs on your head to the details of your toes, every quirk in your personality, even your dreams and desires were created by God for a purpose! You are exactly as He intended!

march

12

creative

So God created mankind in his own image, in the image of God he **created** them; male and female he created them.

Genesis 1:27 (NIV)

. . . .

You, designed by God, are destined for things far beyond your comprehension. The God of the universe made you in His image. Use your God-given gifts and **creativity** for His glory and He will make you a great success!

march

13

credit

For what **credit** is there if, when you sin and are harshly treated, you endure it with patience? But if when you do what is right and suffer for it you patiently endure it, this finds favor with God.

1 Peter 2:20 (NASB)

. . . .

When it is easy to fall into sin, resist the devil. Your God will give you the strength you need to do what is right. Stand firm in the Lord and it will be **credited** to you as righteousness.

march

14

dearly

Therefore, as God's chosen people, holy and **dearly** loved, clothe yourselves with compassion, kindness, humility, gentleness and patience.

Colossians 3:12 (NIV)

. . . .

The love of God is intimate and perfect. You are **dear** to His heart. Show His great love to others by your great compassion, kindness, humility, gentleness and patience, that they may come to know Him.

march

15

decide

Remember this: Whoever sows sparingly will also reap sparingly, and whoever sows generously will also reap generously. Each of you should give what you have **decided** in your heart to give, not reluctantly or under compulsion, for God loves a cheerful giver.

2 Corinthians 9:6–7 (NIV)

. . . .

Give generously, love unconditionally and hope continually. Let your every **decision** be motivated by the love of Christ.

march

16

dedicate

It is a trap to **dedicate** something rashly and only later to consider one's vows.

Proverbs 20:25 (NIV)

. . . .

Avoid making hasty commitments and rushed decisions. **Dedicate** your heart to the Lord and walk in patience. A patient man is never disappointed.

march

deeply

Now that you have purified yourselves by obeying the truth so that you have sincere love for each other, love one another **deeply**, from the heart.

1 Peter 1:22 (NIV)

. . . .

Deeply love your brothers and sisters in Christ. The Bible says there is no greater love than when a man lays down his life for a friend. Just as Christ placed your life before His very own, prefer others before yourself.

march

18

defined

Speaking to the people, he went on, "Take care! Protect yourself against the least bit of greed. Life is not **defined** by what you have, even when you have a lot."

Luke 12:15 (The Message)

. . . .

Your worth is **defined** by Jesus. Greed will not bring wealth, only destruction. Remember, man looks at the outward appearance, but the Lord looks at your heart.

march

19

delicate

You made all the **delicate**, inner parts of my body and knit me together in my mother's womb.

Psalm 139:13 (NLT)

. . . .

How amazing is God's attention to detail! From the **delicate** fingerprints of a newborn baby to the complex thoughts of the human mind . . . God's ways are flawless and unmatched!

delight

Take **delight** in the LORD, and he will give you the desires of your heart.

Psalm 37:4 (NIV)

. . . .

Just as you delight in the Lord, He **delights** in you! Trust in His goodness and the desires He has placed in your heart.

march

21

deliverance

My times are in your hands; **deliver** me from the hands of my enemies, from those who pursue me.

Psalm 31:15 (NIV)

. . . .

Whatever battle you are facing, God is your **Deliverer**. The enemy is no match for His power and presence. Rest on His shoulders and He will carry you to victory!

march

22

detail

The LORD directs the steps of the godly. He delights in every **detail** of their lives.

Psalm 37:23 (NLT)

. . . .

The Lord cares about every area of your life. What matters to you, matters to God. There is no **detail** too small to merit His attention!

march

23

determination

Guard your heart above all else, for it **determines** the course of your life.

Proverbs 4:23 (NLT)

. . . .

Your heart is your most precious possession. Be **determined** to protect it from the evil one. From within your heart, Jesus leads you to His life!

devotion

"No one can serve two masters. Either you will hate the one and love the other, or you will be **devoted** to the one and despise the other. You cannot serve both God and money."

Luke 16:13 (NIV)

. . . .

The Bible says that the "love of money is the root of all evil." The riches of this world are only a distraction from pure **devotion** to Jesus. Serve the Lord with everything and you will lack nothing!

diligence

The plans of the **diligent** lead to profit as surely as haste leads to poverty.

Proverbs 21:5 (NIV)

. . . .

Diligence and patience lead to profit. Riches that are gained quickly disappear. Trust the Lord and you will prosper!

march

26

divine

Through these he has given us his very great and precious promises, so that through them you may participate in the **divine** nature, having escaped the corruption in the world caused by evil desires.

2 Peter 1:4 (NIV)

. . . .

The ways of God are **divine**. You do not have to fall prey to sin and evil. You can walk above the crookedness of this world.

dreams

Hope deferred makes the heart sick, but a **dream** fulfilled is a tree of life.

Proverbs 13:12 (NLT)

. . . .

Your heavenly Father longs to bring your **dreams** to pass even more than you do. Do not lose hope! Just as one door closes, another opens.

march

28

dynamic

Confess to one another therefore your faults (your slips, your false steps, your offenses, your sins) and pray [also] for one another, that you may be healed and restored [to a spiritual tone of mind and heart]. The earnest (heartfelt, continued) prayer of a righteous man makes tremendous power available [**dynamic** in its working].

James 5:16 (AMP)

. . . .

Prayer holds the power to abolish strongholds and set captives free! From here on Earth and up to heaven, it is forceful and **dynamic**. Prayer changes everything!

march

29

eager

A faithful person will be richly blessed, but one **eager** to get rich will not go unpunished.

Proverbs 28:20 (NIV)

. . . .

Always be **eager** for the things of God. His favor, blessing, prosperity and goodness far outweigh the riches of this world. His promises last forever!

march

30

earnestness

And without faith it is impossible to please God, because anyone who comes to him must believe that he exists and that he rewards those who **earnestly** seek him.

Hebrews 11:6 (NIV)

. . . .

The Lord pours out blessings on those who **earnestly** seek Him. Faith isn't faith when we can see exactly what lies ahead. Just believe in the faithfulness of God!

march

31

efficiency

Do you see a person who is **efficient** in his work? He will serve kings. He will not serve unknown people.

Proverbs 22:29 (GW)

. . . .

Whatever work your hands find to do, work as unto the Lord! An **efficient** worker is hard to find, and the reward is great!

elevate

Uprightness and right standing with God (moral and spiritual rectitude in every area and relation) **elevate** a nation, but sin is a reproach to any people.

Proverbs 14:34 (AMP)

. . . .

Sin may be appealing for a moment, but in the end it only brings harm. God **elevates** those who are pure in heart, who live according to His Word, so that others may see and believe!

april

2

eloquence

Moses said to the Lord, "Pardon your servant, Lord. I have never been **eloquent**, neither in the past nor since you have spoken to your servant. I am slow of speech and tongue." The Lord said to him, "Who gave human beings their mouths? Who makes them deaf or mute? Who gives them sight or makes them blind? Is it not I, the Lord?"

Exodus 4:10–11 (NIV)

. . . .

When you minister to others, do not worry about what you will say. **Eloquent** and clever words are pleasant to the ear, but it is the Lord who gives life and power to your words.

april

3

eminent

A gift gets attention; it buys the attention of **eminent** people.

Proverbs 18:16 (The Message)

· ·

Eminence and fame are appealing, but authenticity and sincerity are most important. Ask the Lord to surround you with people and friends of integrity.

april

4

empty

The wise don't engage in **empty** chatter. What good are such words?

Job 15:3 (NLT)

. . . .

Empty words are only a waste of breath. Life and death are in the power of the tongue. Let your mouth speak words of encouragement and life to those around you!

enable

So we keep on praying for you, asking our God to **enable** you to live a life worthy of his call. May he give you the power to accomplish all the good things your faith prompts you to do.

2 Thessalonians 1:11 (NLT)

. . . .

The Lord will give you all that you need to achieve His calling on your life. His strength, power, grace, favor and blessing will **enable** you to rise above every challenge that comes across your path.

april

encourage

Finally, brothers and sisters, rejoice! Strive for full restoration, **encourage** one another, be of one mind, live in peace. And the God of love and peace will be with you.

2 Corinthians 13:11 (NIV)

Today, set out to **encourage** others! If you have a broken relationship, seek understanding, peace and restoration. You will find that you are more blessed than those you bless!

april

7

endurance

We also pray that you will be strengthened with all his glorious power so you will have all the **endurance** and patience you need. May you be filled with joy . . .

Colossians 1:11 (NLT)

. . . .

The Lord wants to fill you with His joy and peace today. His great power will give you all the **endurance** you need to fulfill His purpose. Take comfort in His strength!

april

8

endless

And Jesus said to him, You have answered correctly; do this, and you will live [enjoy active, blessed, **endless** life in the kingdom of God].

Luke 10:28 (AMP)

. . . .

Our days on Earth are numbered, but in Christ we find everlasting life. The Kingdom of God is **endless**. Our minds cannot comprehend the vastness of eternity!

april

9

enlighten

"For You are my lamp, O LORD; The LORD shall **enlighten** my darkness."

2 Samuel 22:29 (NKJV)

. . . .

The **enlightenment** of the Lord brings understanding of His ways. Ask the Lord to shed His light into your situation. He will make His way clear!

enthusiastically

Never be lazy, but work hard and serve the Lord **enthusiastically**.

Romans 12:11 (NLT)

· ·

Approach each day with great expectation and **enthusiasm**. God rewards those who work hard, but laziness brings no profit. In everything you do, do it for the glory of the Lord!

esteem

Choose a good reputation over great riches; being held in high **esteem** is better than silver or gold.

Proverbs 22:1 (NLT)

. . . .

Strive to be a person of great character, full of integrity. Riches will buy you many friends, but when the money is gone so are they! But those who are highly respected and **esteemed** by others will have friends for life!

eternal

The fear of the LORD is the beginning of wisdom; all who follow his precepts have good understanding. To him belongs **eternal** praise.

Psalm 111:10 (NIV)

. . . .

God is the originator of all wisdom and power. His holiness and sovereignty are **eternal**. Worship the Lord without end, for He is worthy of all glory, honor and praise!

exalt

The LORD is my strength and my song; he has given me victory. This is my God, and I will praise him—my father's God, and I will **exalt** him!

Exodus 15:2 (NLT)

. . . .

You have everything you need to walk victoriously in this life. There is great strength found in praising the Lord. **Exalt** Him high above your enemies!

april

14

exceedingly

But let the righteous be glad; let them rejoice before God: yea, let them **exceedingly** rejoice.

Psalm 68:3 (KJV)

. . . .

Your heavenly Father has given you complete righteousness through Christ in exchange for your sin. Live thankfully and praise Him **exceedingly**!

april

excellence

By his divine power, God has given us everything we need for living a godly life. We have received all of this by coming to know him, the one who called us to himself by means of his marvelous glory and **excellence**.

2 Peter 1:3 (NLT)

. . . .

Living a Godly life does not come from your own efforts. A life of **excellence** is the result of a relationship with the Creator of all life. His power within you is the key to a righteous life!

april

16

excitement

Zacchaeus quickly climbed down and took Jesus to his house in great **excitement** and joy.

Luke 19:6 (NLT)

· ·

Be **excited** to share the good news of Jesus with others! He is the only One who gives lasting joy and brings hope to the lost. He is the life that this world is longing for.

experience

May you **experience** the love of Christ, though it is too great to understand fully. Then you will be made complete with all the fullness of life and power that comes from God.

Ephesians 3:19 (NLT)

. . . .

The love of Christ is not just an expression. The love of Christ is a beautiful **experience**, real and life-changing, indescribable and far beyond understanding. May you experience His love today!

april

18

exquisite

How **exquisite** your love, O God! How eager we are to run under your wings, To eat our fill at the banquet you spread as you fill our tankards with Eden spring water. You're a fountain of cascading light, and you open our eyes to light.

Psalm 36:7–9 (The Message)

· ·

Your heavenly Father loves everything about you. His deep love for you is **exquisite**. He has given you unique gifts that only you can use to fulfill His purpose.

april

19

extraordinary

And amazement seized them all, and they glorified God and were filled with awe, saying, "We have seen **extraordinary** things today."

Luke 5:26 (ESV)

. . . .

The Lord gives sight to the blind and hearing to the deaf. He sets captives free from years of bondage and heals the brokenhearted. The works of God are **extraordinary** and too great for our minds to understand!

fairness

Masters, provide your slaves with what is right and **fair**, because you know that you also have a Master in heaven.

Colossians 4:1 (NIV)

. . . .

The Bible says that a man will reap what he sows. Treat others as you would want to be treated. Be a person of integrity, honesty and **fairness**.

april

21

faithfulness

For the word of the LORD is right and true; he is **faithful** in all he does.

Psalm 33:4 (NIV)

. . . .

Your heavenly Father is **faithful** to you even when you are unfaithful. He does not neglect His Word, and His promises are real. Trust in the faithfulness of your God.

fame

. . . and Jesus' brothers said to him, "Leave here and go to Judea, where your followers can see your miracles! You can't become **famous** if you hide like this! If you can do such wonderful things, show yourself to the world!"

John 7:3–4 (NLT)

. . . .

Make the name of Jesus **famous**! Tell others of His great miracles and do not keep Him hidden within your heart. He is a bright light to a dark world.

fasten

Stand therefore, having **fastened** on the belt of truth, and having put on the breastplate of righteousness, and, as shoes for your feet, having put on the readiness given by the gospel of peace.

Ephesians 6:14–15 (ESV)

. . . .

The Word of God contains all the power and strength you need to face your enemy. His truth abolishes every lie and His peace guides your every step. **Fasten** God's Word to your heart.

april

24

faultless

Religion that God our Father accepts as pure and **faultless** is this: to look after orphans and widows in their distress and to keep oneself from being polluted by the world.

James 1:27 (NIV)

. . . .

Believe in Jesus the Savior of the world, love people in your words and actions, and don't give evil a foothold in your life. Manmade religion is not without error, but Jesus is **faultless**!

favor

For his anger lasts only a moment, but his **favor** lasts a life-time; weeping may stay for the night, but rejoicing comes in the morning.

Psalm 30:5 (NIV)

. . . .

The **favor** of the Lord will take you farther than any skill of your own. Honor Him with your life and He will take you to heights you could never imagine. Let Him be your advocate!

april

26

favored

LORD, when you **favored** me, you made my royal mountain stand firm; but when you hid your face, I was dismayed.

Psalm 30:7 (NIV)

. . . .

You are **favored** by God. He chose you as His own from the beginning of time. You are His treasured possession, the work of His hands and an heir of His promises.

fearlessness

They do not fear bad news; they confidently trust the Lord to care for them. They are confident and **fearless** and can face their foes triumphantly.

Psalm 112:7–8 (NLT)

· ·

The Bible says to trust the Lord and not your own understanding. Your situation may look hopeless, but you can walk in **fearlessness** because God is with you. He goes before you and follows after you.

april

28

fearfulness

So you have not received a spirit that makes you **fearful** slaves. Instead, you received God's Spirit when he adopted you as his own children. Now we call him, "Abba, Father."

Romans 8:15 (NLT)

. . . .

God is your Father. He is your Protector, and you do not have to be **fearful** of what is to come. Ask the Holy Spirit to be your Comforter and to bring peace to your heart.

fellowship

May the grace of the Lord Jesus Christ, the love of God, and the **fellowship** of the Holy Spirit be with you all.

2 Corinthians 13:14 (NLT)

. . . .

Fellowship with the Holy Spirit is a precious gift. God gave His Spirit for the comfort and peace of His people and to lead them to His life. Let the Holy Spirit fill and comfort you today!

april

30

fidelity

Exhort servants to be obedient unto their own masters, and to please them well in all things; not answering again; Not purloining, but shewing all good **fidelity**; that they may adorn the doctrine of God our Savior in all things.

Titus 2:9–10 (KJV)

. . . .

Be a person of **fidelity** in all of your relationships. Your heavenly Father will defend you amid the unfaithfulness of others. Trust your relationship with God above any other, for He is faithful!

may

1

ferocity

You forgave the iniquity of your people and covered all their sins. You set aside all your wrath and turned from your **fierce** anger.

Psalm 85:2–3 (NIV)

. . . .

The Lord is capable of great anger, but greater than that anger is the **ferocity** of His love. He loves you with an intense love, full of mercy and forgiveness. His love is immeasurable!

finality

When he had received the drink, Jesus said, "It is **finished**."
With that, he bowed his head and gave up his spirit.

John 19:30 (NIV)

. . . .

The **finality** of Jesus' death on the cross brought redemption
to mankind. Jesus was the ultimate sacrifice, and no other
man could have paid that debt. He is the Savior of the world!

flawlessness

As for God, his way is perfect: The LORD's word is **flawless**; he shields all who take refuge in him.

Psalm 18:30 (NIV)

. . . .

The Bible says there is a way that seems right to man, but in the end it leads to death. Trust in God's ways; they are **flawless** and lead to a righteous life. Follow His lead and He will guard your life.

may

4

forgiveness

When Jesus saw their faith, he said, "Friend, your sins are **forgiven**."

Luke 5:20 (NIV)

．．．．．．．．．．．．．．．．．．．．．．．．．．．．．．．．．．．．．．．

Complete **forgiveness** is yours in Christ Jesus. Every sin in your past and every sin you have yet to commit is wiped away. You are the righteousness of Christ.

may

5

free

So if the Son sets you **free**, you will be free indeed.

John 8:36 (NIV)

. . . .

You are **free** from bondage and captivity. You are free to live, love and laugh. Jesus Christ has set you free and there is not a person on this Earth who can take that away from you.

freedom

"The Spirit of the Lord is on me, because he has anointed me to proclaim good news to the poor. He has sent me to proclaim **freedom** for the prisoners and recovery of sight for the blind, to set the oppressed free, to proclaim the year of the Lord's favor."

Luke 4:18–19 (NIV)

. . . .

There is complete **freedom** in Jesus. Freedom from addiction, pain, sin and sorrow is yours. All you have to do is take hold of it!

may

7

friend

One who loves a pure heart and who speaks with grace will have the king for a **friend**.

Proverbs 22:11 (NIV)

. . . .

You have the best **friend** one could ever hope for in Jesus. He is loving, loyal, gracious, honest and compassionate. You have the King for a friend!

may

8

friendship

For since our **friendship** with God was restored by the death of his Son while we were still his enemies, we will certainly be saved through the life of his Son.

Romans 5:10 (NLT)

. . . .

Friendship is truly a gift from God. Treasure the gift of His friendship and the friendship of those you are closest to; a loyal friend is hard to find.

may

9

fruitfulness

That ye might walk worthy of the Lord unto all pleasing, being **fruitful** in every good work, and increasing in the knowledge of God . . .

Colossians 1:10 (KJV)

. . . .

God determines your success. Work hard and the Lord will make your efforts **fruitful** and rewarding!

fulfillment

Not one of all the LORD's good promises to Israel failed; every one was **fulfilled**.

Joshua 21:45 (NIV)

. . . .

There isn't a single promise the Lord has made that He has not or will not **fulfill**. Trust in His goodness and faithfulness today!

generosity

You will be enriched in every way so that you can be generous on every occasion, and through us your **generosity** will result in thanksgiving to God.

2 Corinthians 9:11 (NIV)

. . . .

God is full of **generosity** for His people. He freely gave His Son to redeem you and all mankind. Praise God for His great love!

gently

Gently instruct those who oppose the truth. Perhaps God will change those people's hearts, and they will learn the truth.

2 Timothy 2:25 (NLT)

. . . .

Respond to opposition in a **gentle** manner. Harsh words only bring about more confrontation. Let kindness rule your tongue, and the Lord will bring the truth to light.

genuine

In all this you greatly rejoice, though now for a little while you may have had to suffer grief in all kinds of trials. These have come so that the proven **genuineness** of your faith—of greater worth than gold, which perishes even though refined by fire—may result in praise, glory and honor when Jesus Christ is revealed.

1 Peter 1:6–7 (NIV)

. . . .

A **genuine** faith in an artificial world is like a candle shining brightly in a dark room. Stand firm, do not lose hope. Your sincere faith brings glory and honor to Jesus Christ!

may

14

gift

For the wages of sin is death, but the **gift** of God is eternal life in Christ Jesus our Lord.

Romans 6:23 (NIV)

. . . .

You have a **gift** to offer the world! Sharing Jesus with the lost and brokenhearted is far greater than anything this world can give.

may

15

gifted

Since you excel in so many ways—in your faith, your **gifted** speakers, your knowledge, your enthusiasm, and your love from us—I want you to excel also in this gracious act of giving.

2 Corinthians 8:7(NLT)

. . . .

The Lord has **gifted** you for great things! His purpose for your life goes beyond your understanding. Ask Him to show you His purpose for the characteristics and talents He has given you.

may

16

given

This is my comfort in my affliction, For Your word has **given** me life.

Psalm 119:50 (NKJV)

. . . .

There is no circumstance in which God will not **give** you the strength to overcome. There is power in His Word. Press into it!

may

godly

It teaches us to say "No" to ungodliness and worldly passions, and to live self-controlled, upright and **godly** lives in this present age, while we wait for the blessed hope—the appearing of the glory of our great God and Savior, Jesus Christ . . .

Titus 2:12–13 (NIV)

. . . .

Let your words and actions reflect the heart of your **God**. Walking in His way is not always easy, but it always results in goodness and favor!

may
18

goodness

I remain confident of this: I will see the **goodness** of the LORD in the land of the living.

Psalm 27:13

. . . .

Your heavenly Father is good to you! The troubles of this life are not easy, but the **goodness** of God is constant. Trust in His unending faithfulness!

may

19

grace

For the law was given through Moses; **grace** and truth came through Jesus Christ.

John 1:17

. . . .

Sin no longer has authority in your life. There is great freedom found when you walk in the **grace** of God. God's amazing grace is the power you need to overcome the temptation of sin!

graceful

Hear, my son, your father's instruction, and forsake not your mother's teaching, for they are a **graceful** garland for your head and pendants for your neck.

Proverbs 1:8–9 (ESV)

. . . .

Do not despise the **graceful** words of those who offer godly wisdom and counsel. Their guidance will protect your life and bring great success.

gracious

But you, Lord, are a compassionate and **gracious** God, slow to anger, abounding in love and faithfulness.

Psalm 86:15 (NIV)

. . . .

God is **gracious** to you! His anger is fierce towards those who love evil, but He is gentle and compassionate towards those who seek to be like Him and long for His ways.

gratification

Rather, clothe yourselves with the Lord Jesus Christ, and do not think about how to **gratify** the desires of the flesh.

Romans 13:14

. . . .

The **gratification** of the flesh produces a temporary pleasure that only brings more emptiness. Instead, satisfy yourself with the beautiful presence of Jesus. He is all the strength you need to overcome your flesh.

may

23

greatly

I delight **greatly** in the LORD; my soul rejoices in my God. For he has clothed me with garments of salvation and arrayed me in a robe of his righteousness, as a bridegroom adorns his head like a priest, and as a bride adorns herself with her jewels.

Isaiah 61:10

. . . .

Delight **greatly** in the Lord today! Let Him be your complete joy. He has given you His righteousness; you can rest in Him.

grown

The path of the lazy man is **grown** over with thorns, but the path of the faithful is a good road.

Proverbs 15:19 (NLV)

. . . .

The Lord doesn't promise that life will be easy, but He does promise to walk it with you. As you **grow** closer to Him, you will see His hand working in every area of your life.

may

25

guidance

For this God is our God for ever and ever; he will be our **guide** even to the end.

Psalm 48:14 (NIV)

. . . .

You can be certain that God will never leave you or forsake you. He will order your steps and **guide** you in the way that is right and true.

guiltless

. . . so that you are not lacking in any gift, as you wait for the revealing of our Lord Jesus Christ, who will sustain you to the end, **guiltless** in the day of our Lord Jesus Christ. God is faithful, by whom you were called into the fellowship of his Son, Jesus Christ our Lord.

1 Corinthians 1:7–9 (ESV)

You are not condemned as a sinner. Because of Jesus, you are found **guiltless** in the eyes of the Lord. Let Him be your identity.

may

27

happiness

Make me walk along the path of your commands, for that is
where my **happiness** is found.

Psalm 119:35 (NLT)

. . . .

God wants you to find **happiness** in Him. The treasures of
this world bring temporary pleasure, but true joy can only
be found in the Lord.

may

28

harmony

Live in **harmony** with each other. Don't be too proud to enjoy the company of ordinary people. And don't think you know it all!

Romans 12:16 (NLT)

. . . .

It pleases the heart of God when we live in **harmony** with those around us. Conflict and arrogance do not bring about blessing, but unity and peace honor the Lord.

may

29

healed

LORD my God, I called to you for help, and you **healed** me.

Psalm 30:2 (NIV)

. . . .

The Lord hears the prayers and desires of your heart. Be full of
hope, for He is your constant Helper and **Healer**.

heartfelt

Perfume and incense bring joy to the heart, and the pleasantness of a friend springs from their **heartfelt** advice.

Proverbs 27:9 (NIV)

. . . .

A true friend will offer sound, life-giving counsel. Their encouragement and **heartfelt** words will bring peace to your spirit.

heavenly

Now this I know: The LORD gives victory to his anointed. He answers him from his **heavenly** sanctuary with the victorious power of his right hand.

Psalm 20:6 (NIV)

· ·

Your **heavenly** Father holds all power and victory over darkness. He answers the cries of His children. You are the treasure of His heart.

june

helper

The LORD is with me; he is my **helper**. I look in triumph on my enemies.

Psalm 118:7 (NIV)

. . . .

With the help of man, tasks are accomplished, but with the **help** of the Lord, the impossible is achieved. Call on the Lord to be your Helper today. He knows no defeat!

june

2

heroic

The Lord your God is with you. He is a **hero** who saves you. He happily rejoices over you, renews you with his love, and celebrates over you with shouts of joy.

Zephaniah 3:17 (GW)

. . . .

The Lord wants to be your **hero**! His strength and power know no limit. He rescues those He loves and He rejoices over you.

june

3

highly

For by the grace given me I say to every one of you: Do not think of yourself more **highly** than you ought, but rather think of yourself with sober judgment, in accordance with the faith God has distributed to each of you.

Romans 12:3 (NIV)

. . . .

Jesus said that the last shall be first and the first shall be last. Hold others above yourself, but most importantly, **highly** exalt Jesus!

holiness

Worship the LORD in the splendor of his **holiness**; tremble before him, all the earth.

Psalm 96:9 (NIV)

. . . .

Stand in awe of all that God has done on your behalf. His **holiness** is without comparison. There is none so glorious as He!

honest

An **honest** answer is like a kiss on the lips.

Proverbs 24:26 (NIV)

. . . .

Be **honest** in your relationships with others. Lies bring distrust and disappointment. The truth may sting for a moment, but in the end it will bring you favor.

honorable

It is God's will that you should be sanctified: that you should avoid sexual immorality; that each of you should learn to control your own body in a way that is holy and **honorable** . . .

1 Thessalonians 4:3–4 (NIV)

. . . .

Esteem the Lord and live in a way that is **honorable** to Him. There is freedom found in His ways. Rejoice in His precepts, for they will protect your life.

june

honor

For the LORD God is a sun and shield; the LORD bestows favor and **honor**; no good thing does he withhold from those whose walk is blameless.

Psalm 84:11 (NIV)

. . . .

Bring glory to the Lord in every area of your life. Exalt the Lord in your relationships, your finances, your body and your faith. Honor Him, and He will **honor** you.

june

8

hope

Guide me in your truth and teach me, for you are God my Savior, and my **hope** is in you all day long.

Psalm 25:5 (NIV)

. . . .

There is no **hope** without Jesus. Because of His great love, He has filled our lives with purpose, truth and promise.

hopeful

Love never gives up, never loses faith, is always **hopeful**, and endures through every circumstance.

1 Corinthians 13:7 (NLT)

. . . .

Be **hopeful** for the days ahead. Your Father in heaven loves you with an unconditional love. No matter what you have done or what you will do, His love never waivers!

june

10

hospitable

Be **hospitable** to one another without grumbling.

1 Peter 4:9 (NKJV)

. . . .

Whatever you do, let love be your motivation. Be generous and **hospitable**, compassionate and joyful towards others and it will bring you happiness!

june

11

humbled

"For all those who exalt themselves will be **humbled**, and those who humble themselves will be exalted."

Luke 14:11 (NIV)

. . . .

The Lord will honor those who are truly **humble** in His eyes. Let the mouths of others compliment you, not your own mouth.

humility

When pride comes, then comes disgrace, but with **humility** comes wisdom.

Proverbs 11:2 (NIV)

. . . .

Let God defend your cause, and He will bring the truth to light. Walk in **humility** before others, seek the Lord's wisdom and there you will find blessing and favor.

june

13

immeasurable

So that in the coming ages he might show the **immeasurable** riches of his grace in kindness toward us in Christ Jesus.

Ephesians 2:7 (ESV)

. . . .

Praise your heavenly Father for His **immeasurable** grace, for if we could count it we would have no hope. His great kindness cannot be matched!

june

14

impressive

Don't be **impressed** with your own wisdom. Instead, fear the
LORD and turn away from evil.

Proverbs 3:7 (NLT)

. . . .

The wisdom of man pales in comparison to the wisdom of
God. Seek the Lord and His righteousness and He will **impress**
His wisdom upon your heart.

june

15

included

And you also were **included** in Christ when you heard the message of truth, the gospel of your salvation. When you believed, you were marked in him with a seal, the promised Holy Spirit . . .

Ephesians 1:13 (NIV)

. . . .

You are **included** in all of the good promises of God! Jesus is your righteousness, the Holy Spirit your comforter, and not one of God's promises will go unfulfilled in your life.

june

16

increase

The law was brought in so that the trespass might **increase**. But where sin increased, grace increased all the more . . .

Romans 5:20 (NIV)

. . . .

As His child, the more you sin, the more grace God shows you! God's love for you is not based on your behavior. His love will not **increase** or decrease—because His love for you is complete now!

incredible

I also pray that you will understand the **incredible** greatness of God's power for us who believe him. This is the same mighty power that raised Christ from the dead and seated him in the place of honor at God's right hand in the heavenly realms.

Ephesians 1:19–20 (NLT)

. . . .

Think about the **incredible** power of your God. He raises the dead to life and gives sight to the blind. And He gave His only Son so that you might spend eternity with Him!

infallible

. . . to whom He also presented Himself alive after His suffering by many **infallible** proofs, being seen by them during forty days and speaking of the things pertaining to the kingdom of God.

Acts 1:3 (NKJV)

. . . .

God's Word is **infallible**! The life of Jesus was perfect. Nothing pertaining to God will ever be proven false.

june

19

infinite

Yes, everything else is worthless when compared with the **infinite** value of knowing Christ Jesus my Lord. For his sake I have discarded everything else, counting it all as garbage, so that I could gain Christ.

Philippians 3:8 (NLT)

. . . .

The worth of knowing Christ is **infinite**, without end, measureless, unfathomable and unsurpassable. There is no treasure so great!

june

20

influence

They share freely and give generously to those in need. Their good deeds will be remembered forever. They will have **influence** and honor.

Psalm 112:9 (NLT)

. . . .

The Lord gives **influence** to those who will use it to bless others and honor Him. Seek to be like Jesus and watch doors of opportunity open!

june

21

insight

How much better to get wisdom than gold, to get **insight** rather than silver!

Proverbs 16:16 (NIV)

. . . .

Ask the Lord to give you **insight** and understanding of His Word. Sometimes the words on the page are confusing, but the Holy Spirit will open your eyes to His truth.

inspire

Those who live at the ends of the earth stand in awe of your wonders. From where the sun rises to where it sets, you **inspire** shouts of joy.

Psalm 65:8 (NLT)

. . . .

Your heavenly Father wants to be your **inspiration**, the source of all your joy. He longs to reveal Himself in your weaknesses.

june

23

intimate

He who conceals a transgression seeks love, But he who repeats a matter separates **intimate** friends.

Proverbs 17:9 (NASB)

. . . .

Intimate and truthful friendships are rare. Do not expose the weaknesses of those you love to others, but instead, protect and cherish them.

june

24

invincible

Who is the King of glory? The LORD, strong and mighty; the LORD, **invincible** in battle.

Psalm 24:8 (NLT)

. . . .

The enemy finds your God unyielding and **invincible**. Do not stand in fear when trouble finds you because God has already won!

june

25

joy

The LORD is my strength and my shield; my heart trusts in him, and he helps me. My heart leaps for **joy**, and with my song I praise him.

Psalm 28:7 (NIV)

. . . .

Take hold of the unexplainable **joy** that comes from the Lord. He wants to be your delight even in the midst of trying times. Trust Him!

june

26

joyful

Be **joyful** in hope, patient in affliction, faithful in prayer.

Romans 12:12 (NIV)

. . . .

You have a reason to always be **joyful** because Jesus has given you hope for the future. He has promised to stand by your side in battle and He will always answer your prayers.

june

27

jubilant

Shout for joy to the LORD, all the earth, burst into **jubilant** song with music . . .

Psalm 98:4 (NIV)

. . . .

Jubilantly sing to the Lord! With great enthusiasm and excitement, make His name famous!

june

28

justified

For all have sinned and fall short of the glory of God, and all are **justified** freely by his grace through the redemption that came by Christ Jesus.

Romans 3:23–24 (NIV)

. . . .

You are not **justified** by any man other than Jesus Christ. Place your confidence in the One whose grace has redeemed you from death!

june

29

keen

The Lord is my Rock, my Fortress, and my Deliverer; my God, my **keen** and firm Strength in Whom I will trust and take refuge, my Shield, and the Horn of my salvation, my High Tower.

Psalm 18:2 (AMP)

. . . .

The Holy Spirit will give you **keen** and deep insight into God's Word. Ask the Holy Spirit to open the eyes of your heart to understand God's perfect ways.

june

30

kindhearted

A **kindhearted** woman gains honor, but ruthless men gain only wealth.

Proverbs 11:16 (NIV)

. . . .

Always seek to be **kindhearted** and compassionate towards others. The Lord will honor you when you love others as He loves you.

july

kindness

Sin ruled by means of death. But God's **kindness** now rules, and God has accepted us because of Jesus Christ our Lord. This means that we will have eternal life.

Romans 5:21 (CEV)

· ·

Let the **kindness** of God reign in your heart today. Demonstrate God's grace to all people, for He has not held your sin against you.

july

2

kissed

Unfailing love and truth have met together. Righteousness and peace have **kissed**!

Psalm 85:10 (NLT)

. . . .

We have peace with God through the righteousness of Christ. Righteousness and peace **kissed** when Jesus came to Earth on behalf of mankind and united God and man. What a beautiful encounter!

knowledge

You hem me in behind and before, and you lay your hand upon me. Such **knowledge** is too wonderful for me, too lofty for me to attain.

Psalm 139:5–6 (NIV)

. . . .

From beginning to end, the Lord holds your life in His hands. Your mind cannot understand His ways and it is incapable of comprehending all of His goodness and **knowledge**.

july

4

known

You make **known** to me the path of life; you will fill me with joy in your presence, with eternal pleasures at your right hand.

Psalm 16:11 (NIV)

. . . .

Do not lose hope when your direction seems unclear. The Lord promises to make His way **known** to you! Remember, His way brings peace to your spirit.

july

5

lavish

How great is the goodness you have stored up for those who fear you. You **lavish** it on those who come to you for protection, blessing them before the watching world.

Psalm 31:19 (NLT)

Your heavenly Father longs to **lavish** His goodness and love on you! He does not withhold anything good from those who seek His heart and live according to His Word.

july

6

liberally

If any of you lacks wisdom, let him ask of God, who gives to all **liberally** and without reproach, and it will be given to him.

James 1:5 (NKJV)

. . . .

God does not show favoritism among believers. He gives wisdom and understanding freely to anyone who asks Him. The Lord **liberally** blesses His people!

liberty

Now the Lord is the Spirit; and where the Spirit of the Lord is, there is **liberty**.

2 Corinthians 3:17 (ASV)

. . . .

There is no feeling comparable to finding freedom in Jesus. The Holy Spirit breaks the chains of addiction and bondage. **Liberty** is yours!

july

8

life

For God so loved the world that he gave his one and only Son, that whoever believes in him shall not perish but have eternal **life**.

John 3:16 (NIV)

. . . .

This world is looking for what is real and genuine. They are searching to quench a thirst that only God can satisfy. Jesus is **life**!

light

Your word is a lamp for my feet, a **light** on my path.

Psalm 119:105 (NIV)

. . . .

Often times you may feel like you are walking in the midst of complete darkness. Let God's Word bring **light** to your surroundings. His Word is truth no matter your circumstances.

july

10

liked

Those who correct others will later be **liked** more than those who give false praise.

Proverbs 28:23 (NCV)

· ·

In the end, your friends will appreciate honesty more than an insincere compliment. Ultimately, good character is **liked** far beyond a flattering tongue.

july

11

longed

"But blessed are your eyes, because they see; and your ears, because they hear. I tell you the truth, many prophets and righteous people longed to see what you see, but they didn't see it. And they **longed** to hear what you hear, but they didn't hear it."

Matthew 13:16–17 (NLT)

. . . .

Place the desires of your heart at the feet of Jesus and rest in Him. Delight yourself in the Lord and He will grant you the **longings** of your heart.

july

12

loosed

"I will give you the keys of the kingdom of heaven; whatever
you bind on earth will be bound in heaven, and whatever you
loose on earth will be **loosed** in heaven."

Matthew 16:19 (NIV)

· ·

You have great authority in Jesus Christ. You hold the power
to **loosen** those who are trapped in darkness and to thwart
the purposes of the enemy!

july

13

loved

"As the Father has loved me, so have I **loved** you. Now remain in my love."

John 15:9 (NIV)

. . . .

You are unconditionally **loved** by your heavenly Father. Rest in His love, walk in His love and rejoice in His love!

july

14

lovely

Praise the LORD, for the LORD is good; celebrate his **lovely** name with music.

Psalm 135:3 (NLT)

. . . .

The Lord is altogether **lovely**. His ways are beautiful and perfect. Praise His wonderful name!

july

15

loyal

Create in me a clean heart, O God. Renew a **loyal** spirit with-in me.

Psalm 51:10 (NLT)

. . . .

Even when your heart strays from God, you can know that He will always be **loyal** to you. He promises that when you seek Him, you will find Him with arms wide open.

july
16

madly

I love you more than I can say. Because I'm **madly** in love with you, they blame me for everything they dislike about you.

Psalm 69:9 (The Message)

. . . .

Your heavenly Father could not love you any more than He already does. He adores you. His every thought is of you and He is **madly** in love with you!

july

17

magnify

I will praise the name of God with a song, And will **magnify** Him with thanksgiving.

Psalm 69:30 (NKJV)

. . . .

Magnify the name of the Lord! Sing His praises every day. Thank Him for His overwhelming goodness.

july

18

majestic

LORD, our Lord, how **majestic** is your name in all the earth!

Psalm 8:9 (NIV)

. . . .

Stand in awe of God's splendor and praise His **majestic** name! Earth proclaims the glory of the Lord!

majesty

The LORD reigns, he is robed in majesty; the LORD is robed in **majesty** and armed with strength; indeed, the world is established, firm and secure.

Psalm 93:1 (NIV)

. . . .

Even the mountains, in all their **majesty**, do not compare to the beauty of the Lord. His glory is beyond compare and His radiance is too bright for human eyes.

july 20

manifest

But Isaiah is very bold and says: "I was found by those who did not seek Me; I was made **manifest** to those who did not ask for Me."

Romans 10:20 (NKJV)

. . . .

The Lord wants to **manifest** Himself in your family, your finances, your health—every area of your life. Ask Him to reveal Himself to you in new ways!

july

21

marked

Therefore, since we are surrounded by such a great cloud of witnesses, let us throw off everything that hinders and the sin that so easily entangles. And let us run with perseverance the race **marked** out for us . . .

Hebrews 12:1 (NIV)

. . . .

You are a child of the Most High God, **marked** by the King of Kings. He has a unique purpose and plan for your life.

july

22

married

But a **married** man has to think about his earthly responsibilities and how to please his wife.

1 Corinthians 7:33 (NLT)

. . . .

Whether you are single or **married**, let the Lord be your contentment. He is the only One who truly satisfies the longings of your heart.

marvelous

But even before I was born, God chose me and called me by his **marvelous** grace.

Galatians 1:15 (NLT)

. . . .

Everything about the Lord is **marvelous**! You cannot fathom the depth of His love for you or the magnitude of His goodness. You have been chosen by God to accomplish great things!

july

24

matchless

They will celebrate and sing about your **matchless** mercy and your power to save.

Psalm 145:7 (CEV)

. . . .

God's mercy is undeserved, yet He lavishes it on His children. He saves all who cry out to Him in desperation. His mercy is **matchless**!

july

25

mature

. . . until we all reach unity in the faith and in the knowledge of the Son of God and become **mature**, attaining to the whole measure of the fullness of Christ.

Ephesians 4:13 (NIV)

. . . .

The pursuit of Christ is lifelong. We are constantly learning and **maturing** in Him. Seek understanding and wisdom every day; long for His presence morning and evening!

july

26

merciful

Hear my voice when I call, LORD; be **merciful** to me and answer me.

Psalm 27:7 (NIV)

. . . .

The Lord is **merciful** and compassionate towards you. His heart breaks when your heart is aching. Call out to Him and He will answer!

july

27

mighty

Finally, be strong in the Lord and in his **mighty** power.

Ephesians 6:10 (NIV)

. . . .

Mighty, powerful, strong, absolute and victorious is the Lord! He has given you His strength for battle and you are not alone; with Him, you win!

july

28

mindful

When I consider your heavens, the work of your fingers, the moon and the stars, which you have set in place, what is mankind that you are **mindful** of them, human beings that you care for them?

Psalm 8:3–4 (NIV)

. . . .

Your Father in heaven is **mindful** of you, and not a moment goes by when He is not thinking of you. Amid all the majesty of creation, you are His treasured possession!

july

29

miraculous

"But if I do his work, believe in the evidence of the **miraculous** works I have done, even if you don't believe me. Then you will know and understand that the Father is in me, and I am in the Father."

John 10:38 (NLT)

· ·

Expect the Lord to do **miraculous** things in your life! He is the God of the impossible, and there is no task too big for Him.

july

30

modest

And I want women to be **modest** in their appearance. They should wear decent and appropriate clothing and not draw attention to themselves by the way they fix their hair or by wearing gold or pearls or expensive clothes. For women who claim to be devoted to God should make themselves attractive by the good things they do.

1 Timothy 2:9–10 (NLT)

. . . .

Men and women, be **modest** and do not think your worth is determined by your outward appearance. The Bible says that man looks on the outside, but the Lord looks at the heart. Let your value and worth be found in Jesus!

july

31

more

I tell you that in the same way there will be **more** rejoicing in heaven over one sinner who repents than over ninety-nine righteous persons who do not need to repent.

Luke 15:7 (NIV)

. . . .

The Bible says that Christ did not come to save the righteous, but the sinner. It also says that where sin is present, even **more** grace abounds!

august

1

motivation

Then I observed that most people are **motivated** to success because they envy their neighbors. But this, too, is meaningless—like chasing the wind.

Ecclesiastes 4:4 (NLT)

. . . .

Let love be the **motivation** in your heart for all things. Love God and love people, then you will find true success!

august

moved

But know this first of all, that no prophecy of Scripture is a matter of one's own interpretation, for no prophecy was ever made by an act of human will, but men **moved** by the Holy Spirit spoke from God.

2 Peter 1:20–21 (NASB)

. . . .

When you are **moved** by the Holy Spirit, there is great peace in where He leads you. Following His lead may not always be easy, but the peace that floods your heart will be beyond your understanding.

august

3

mysteries

He reveals deep and **mysterious** things and knows what lies hidden in darkness, though he is surrounded by light.

Daniel 2:22 (NLT)

. . . .

The ways of God are **mysterious** and complex. Even though your eyes cannot see beyond the darkness, rest in knowing that nothing is hidden from the Lord. Trust in His ways!

near

Come near to God and he will come **near** to you. Wash your hands, you sinners, and purify your hearts, you double-minded.

James 4:8 (NIV)

. . . .

Your heavenly Father longs to be **near** to you! He longs to reveal Himself to you. Draw close to Him and let Him purify your heart.

august

new

"See, the former things have taken place, and **new** things I declare; before they spring into being I announce them to you."

Isaiah 42:9 (NIV)

. . . .

God wants to do a **new** work in your life! The past is done and gone. Great things are coming!

august

6

noble

But the seed on good soil stands for those with a **noble** and good heart, who hear the word, retain it, and by persevering produce a crop.

Luke 8:15 (NIV)

. . . .

Be a person of admirable and **noble** character. Stand firm in the Word of God and let your character portray His heart.

august

7

nourishment

Now therefore fear ye not: I will **nourish** you, and your little ones. And he comforted them, and spake kindly unto them.

Genesis 50:21 (KJV)

· ·

Just as an earthly father wants to provide **nourishing** food for his children, your heavenly Father promises to provide for you. He knows your needs—physical and spiritual. Trust Him to provide!

august

8

numerous

So we, **numerous** as we are, are one body in Christ (the Messiah) and individually we are parts one of another [mutually dependent on one another].

Romans 12:5 (AMP)

. . . .

We in the body of Christ should always build up and encourage one another. And though we are great in **number**, seek unity. Join together to represent Christ's love to the world!

august

9

nurture

And, ye fathers, provoke not your children to wrath: but bring them up in the **nurture** and admonition of the Lord.

Ephesians 6:4 (KJV)

. . . .

Nurture those you love in the integrity, purity, wisdom and counsel of the Lord. Lead them to the only One who gives true life.

august

10

obey

Children, **obey** your parents in everything, for this pleases the Lord.

Colossians 3:20 (NIV)

. . . .

No matter what season of life you are in, **obedience** is greatly rewarded by God. Honor those who have been given authority over you and the Lord will promote you further than you ever imagined.

august

11

obtain

Plans are established by seeking advice; so if you wage war, **obtain** guidance.

Proverbs 20:18 (NIV)

. . . .

The Bible says plans succeed when there are many advisors. There is great wisdom and peace found in **obtaining** counsel.

offer

Do not offer any part of yourself to sin as an instrument of wickedness, but rather offer yourselves to God as those who have been brought from death to life; and **offer** every part of yourself to him as an instrument of righteousness.

Romans 6:13 (NIV)

....

Offer everything you have to Jesus, the good and the bad. He will turn your weakness into strength, your sorrow into joy and your sin into righteousness. He wants to use you!

omnipotent

This is the [Lord's] purpose that is purposed upon the whole earth [regarded as conquered and put under tribute by Assyria]; and this is [His **omnipotent**] hand that is stretched out over all the nations.

Isaiah 14:26 (AMP)

. . . .

You have the **omnipotent** God on your side, and He promises to never leave. He gives overwhelming strength and power to those who call on His name.

opportunity

Therefore, as we have **opportunity**, let us do good to all people, especially to those who belong to the family of believers.

Galatians 6:10 (NIV)

. . . .

Take every **opportunity** to bless someone else. In blessing others, you are blessed. There is an unexplainable joy that comes in giving life to those around you!

ordain

Your eyes saw my unformed body; all the days **ordained** for me were written in your book before one of them came to be.

Psalm 139:16 (NIV)

. . . .

From the day of your birth until the day you go to heaven, God has **ordained** all of your days. He knows the great ones and the tough ones, the joyous ones and the sad ones. And He is with you always!

august

16

original

But exhort one another every day, as long as it is called "today," that none of you may be hardened by the deceitfulness of sin. For we have come to share in Christ, if indeed we hold our **original** confidence firm to the end.

Hebrews 3:13–14 (ESV)

. . . .

Do not let the sins of this world distract you from the **original** confidence you had in Christ. Encourage your brothers and sisters in Christ and God will give you the strength you need to remain steadfast.

august

17

over

Do not forsake wisdom, and she will protect you; love her, and she will watch **over** you.

Proverbs 4:6 (NIV)

. . . .

Walking in wisdom is not always easy. Often it means giving up something temporary to obtain something eternal. Desire wisdom **over** riches or any other thing.

pardoned

"Do not judge, and you will not be judged; and do not condemn, and you will not be condemned; **pardon**, and you will be pardoned."

Luke 6:37 (NASB)

. . . .

Show grace to others and your heavenly Father will show immeasurable grace to you. All your sins have been **pardoned**; live to show others the same mercy that has been shown to you.

august

19

passion

The LORD examines the righteous, but the wicked, those who love violence, he hates with a **passion**.

Psalm 11:5 (NIV)

. . . .

God loves with a **passion** and He hates with a passion! Through Jesus Christ, you have been made righteous in the eyes of the Lord. God loves you passionately!

august

20

patient

Whoever is **patient** has great understanding, but one who is quick-tempered displays folly.

Proverbs 14:29 (NIV)

. . . .

Be **patient** and wait on the Lord. If you rush, you will only end up disappointed. God has the best for you in His timing!

august

21

peaceful

A **peaceful** heart leads to a healthy body; jealousy is like cancer in the bones.

Proverbs 14:30 (NLT)

. . . .

A person whose heart is at peace brings life to themselves and everyone around them. Be confident and at rest in God's plans and purpose for your life. **Peaceful** are the ways of the Lord.

perfected

Though He was a Son, yet He learned obedience by the things which He suffered. And having been **perfected**, He became the author of eternal salvation to all who obey Him . . .

Hebrews 5:8–9 (NKJV)

. . . .

You will never achieve **perfection** on your own. But you can trust in Jesus, the One who is perfect all of the time!

august

23

persevere

You need to **persevere** so that when you have done the will of God, you will receive what he has promised.

Hebrews 10:36 (NIV)

. . . .

Great character is established as you **persevere** in all that God has called you to. Do not give up or lose hope, the promises of God are trustworthy and certain.

august

24

persistent

To those who by **persistence** in doing good seek glory, honor and immortality, he will give eternal life.

Romans 2:7 (NIV)

. . . .

Be **persistent**; remain faithful and pursue the things of God. Doors of opportunity do not always open on the first knock . . . keep knocking.

august

25

pleasant

For wisdom will enter your heart, and knowledge will be **pleasant** to your soul.

Proverbs 2:10 (NIV)

. . . .

Open your heart to the wisdom and knowledge of God. His ways bring peace and He will lead you down **pleasant** paths.

plenty

I know what it is to be in need, and I know what it is to have **plenty**. I have learned the secret of being content in any and every situation, whether well fed or hungry, whether living in plenty or in want.

Philippians 4:12 (NIV)

. . . .

Your heavenly Father wants you to be content in Him, no matter the state of your circumstances. Whether you have **plenty** or lack much, He will always be everything you need!

august

27

poised

Do you know how God controls the clouds and makes his lightning flash? Do you know how the clouds hang **poised**, those wonders of him who has perfect knowledge?

Job 37:15–16 (NIV)

. . . .

Remain **poised**, ready to answer the call of the Lord. Whatever your hopes and dreams, prepare yourself for the day when the Lord will bring them about. Be ready!

august

28

powerful

The Son is the radiance of God's glory and the exact representation of his being, sustaining all things by his **powerful** word. After he had provided purification for sins, he sat down at the right hand of the Majesty in heaven.

Hebrews 1:3 (NIV)

. . . .

The Word of God is your authority over evil, **powerful** enough to pierce through any darkness. Immerse yourself in His Word and be amazed at the fruit it produces in your life!

a good word for a great day! | 365 daily inspirations

august

29

practice

"But the one who hears my words and does not put them into **practice** is like a man who built a house on the ground without a foundation. The moment the torrent struck that house, it collapsed and its destruction was complete."

Luke 6:49 (NIV)

. . . .

The Bible says faith without works is dead. **Practice** loving and serving others. Put action to your words!

august

30

praise

I will **praise** the LORD, who counsels me; even at night my heart instructs me.

Psalm 16:7 (NIV)

. . . .

Cultivating a heart of **praise** opens you to hearing the voice of God. **Fall asleep with His praises on your lips and He'll impart wisdom, even as you sleep!**

august

31

prayerful

After Jesus said this, he looked toward heaven and **prayed**: "Father, the hour has come. Glorify your Son, that your Son may glorify you."

John 17:1 (NIV)

. . . .

Remain **prayerful** through difficult times, for this will bring glory to your Father in heaven. Believe in the goodness of your God even when the circumstances appear hopeless.

september

present

Now if we are children, then we are heirs—heirs of God and co-heirs with Christ, if indeed we share in his sufferings in order that we may also share in his glory. I consider that our **present** sufferings are not worth comparing with the glory that will be revealed in us.

Romans 8:17–18 (NIV)

. . . .

Be careful not to get caught up in your **present** circumstances. Your God is the God of yesterday, today and forever. He sees the bigger picture and He will provide a way for you!

september

2

prized

Whatever is good and perfect comes down to us from God our Father, who created all the lights in the heavens. He never changes or casts a shifting shadow. He chose to give birth to us by giving us his true word. And we, out of all creation, became his **prized** possession.

James 1:17–18 (NLT)

. . . .

Think about this . . . you are God's **prized** possession! He takes delight in you as His child. You do not belong to the world, but you are an heir of the Lord!

september

3

produce

My dear brothers and sisters, take note of this: Everyone should be quick to listen, slow to speak and slow to become angry, because human anger does not **produce** the righteousness that God desires.

James 1:19–20 (NIV)

. . . .

The Bible says that a good tree bears good fruit and a bad tree bears bad fruit. Fill yourself with the Word of God so your heart **produces** good things.

september

prompt

With this in mind, we constantly pray for you, that our God may make you worthy of his calling, and that by his power he may bring to fruition your every desire for goodness and your every deed **prompted** by faith.

2 Thessalonians 1:11 (NIV)

. . . .

Lay your desires at the feet of Jesus and surrender to His calling. May you be motivated by love and **prompted** by the Holy Spirit to follow as He leads.

september

5

prosper

A generous person will **prosper**; whoever refreshes others will be refreshed.

Proverbs 11:25 (NIV)

. . . .

A selfish person does not live a blessed life. Make it your goal to encourage and uplift others and the Lord will **prosper** you!

september

6

protected

It was the LORD our God himself who brought us and our parents up out of Egypt, from that land of slavery, and performed those great signs before our eyes. He **protected** us on our entire journey and among all the nations through which we traveled.

Joshua 24:17 (NIV)

. . . .

In this world, you will have trouble, but the Lord is your **Protector**. He will guard your way and defend your cause because you are His child.

september

7

proud

Love is patient, love is kind. It does not envy, it does not boast, it is not **proud**.

1 Corinthians 13:4 (NIV)

· ·

Walk in love for others rather than being **proud** or demeaning. God's love for you is unconditional. In this same way, love others regardless of their condition, or yours.

september

purity

Don't let anyone look down on you because you are young,
but set an example for the believers in speech, in conduct, in
love, in faith and in **purity**.

1 Timothy 4:12 (NIV)

. . . .

Your heart has been cleansed, made new by Jesus Christ. Now
walk in the **purity** you have been given. Let your words and
actions bring Him glory!

september

9

pursue

Turn from evil and do good; seek peace and **pursue** it.

Psalm 34:14 (NIV)

. . . .

Whatever the cost, **pursue** peace with those around you. The Bible says that if possible, you should live at peace with all men.

qualified

It is not that we think we are qualified to do anything on our own. Our **qualification** comes from God.

2 Corinthians 3:5 (NLT)

. . . .

You can't **qualify** yourself for the righteousness of Christ. Jesus gave you His righteousness as a gift, and in Him you stand blameless before the Father.

quickened

For Christ also hath once suffered for sins, the just for the unjust, that he might bring us to God, being put to death in the flesh, but **quickened** by the Spirit . . .

1 Peter 3:18 (KJV)

. . . .

Because you are in Christ, you have been given the Holy Spirit. You no longer have to operate in the flesh. You are **quickened** and led by the Spirit of God.

quieted

But I have calmed and **quieted** myself, I am like a weaned child
with its mother; like a weaned child I am content.

Psalm 131:2 (NIV)

. . . .

Quiet yourself before the Lord. Make time to sit in His presence
and let Him flood your heart with His love.

september

13

quietly

Let all that I am wait **quietly** before God, for my hope is in him.

Psalm 62:5 (NLT)

. . . .

Often the Lord speaks **quietly** to your heart and not as roaring thunder from the heavens. Seek to know His voice so that even in the midst of many voices, you will know His whisper.

september

14

quietness

The fruit of that righteousness will be peace; its effect will be **quietness** and confidence forever. My people will live in peaceful dwelling places, in secure homes, in undisturbed places of rest.

Isaiah 32:17–18 (NIV)

. . . .

When you are waiting on the promises of God, wait patiently. In **quietness** and confidence seek His face and place all of your hope in His Word.

september

15

radiant

The precepts of the LORD are right, giving joy to the heart. The commands of the LORD are **radiant**, giving light to the eyes.

Psalm 19:8 (NIV)

. . . .

The Lord wants to fill you up with Himself so that you are **radiant** and full of His glory. The smallest bit of His light can penetrate the darkness.

september

radical

"God overlooks it as long as you don't know any better—but that time is past. The unknown is now known, and he's calling for a **radical** life-change. He has set a day when the entire human race will be judged and everything set right. And he has already appointed the judge, confirming him before everyone by raising him from the dead."

Acts 17:30–31 (The Message)

. . . .

You cannot, on your own, **radically** change the course of your life. God's power is the strength to walk away from the things of your past and the hope to move toward your future.

september

17

rarely

Very **rarely** will anyone die for a righteous person, though for a good person someone might possibly dare to die.

Romans 5:7 (NIV)

. . . .

Rare are those who would die for the cause of Christ. You will come across those who persecute your faith, but consider it a joy when you must stand up for Jesus!

september

18

ravishingly

There's no one like her on earth, never has been, never will be. She's a woman beyond compare. My dove is perfection, Pure and innocent as the day she was born, and cradled in joy by her mother. Everyone who came by to see her exclaimed and admired her—All the fathers and mothers, the neighbors and friends, blessed and praised her: "Has anyone ever seen anything like this—dawn-fresh, moon-lovely, sun-radiant, **ravishing** as the night sky with its galaxies of stars?"

Song of Solomon 6:8–10 (The Message)

Beautiful, lovely, **ravishing** and magnificent are God's creations. From the snow covered mountains to the depth of the stars, to the complexity of man and woman, His work is glorious!

september

realistic

As for you, the anointing you received from him remains in you, and you do not need anyone to teach you. But as his anointing teaches you, about all things and as that anointing is **real**, not counterfeit—just as it has taught you, remain in him.

1 John 2:27 (NIV)

. . . .

People recognize authenticity. The anointing of Christ is on you, and you have **real** faith and true life to offer the world. Don't hold back!

realized

I **realized** that no one can discover everything God is doing under the sun. Not even the wisest people discover everything, no matter what they claim.

Ecclesiastes 8:17 (NLT)

. . . .

God is always present and always working. You must **realize** that He sees the bigger picture. Trust His wisdom and ways.

september

receive

Though my father and mother forsake me, the LORD will **receive** me.

Psalm 27:10 (NIV)

. . . .

Your heavenly Father **receives** you with open arms. Regardless of your past, He fully accepts you just as you are.

september

22

redeemed

Christ has **redeemed** us from the curse of the law, having become a curse for us (for it is written, "Cursed is everyone who hangs on a tree").

Galatians 3:13 (NKJV)

. . . .

You are **redeemed** by the blood of Jesus Christ. The sin you once carried now hangs on the cross. The righteousness of Christ and the grace of God are yours!

refined

And the words of the LORD are flawless, like silver purified in a crucible, like gold **refined** seven times.

Psalm 12:6 (NIV)

. . . .

Gold is **refined** until it is in its purest form. In the same way, the Lord wants to refine you again and again to become more like Him.

september

24

refreshed

I sleep and wake up **refreshed** because you, LORD, protect me.

Psalm 3:5 (CEV)

. . . .

The Word of the Lord is **refreshing**. His Word breathes new life into your spirit. He is the Restorer!

september

25

refuge

But let all who take **refuge** in you be glad; let them ever sing for joy. Spread your protection over them, that those who love your name may rejoice in you.

Psalm 5:11 (NIV)

. . . .

The Lord is your security and **refuge**. Run into His arms when trouble comes. Praise Him for His protection!

september

26

relationship

No one has ever seen God, but the one and only Son, who is himself God and is in closest **relationship** with the Father, has made him known.

John 1:18 (NIV)

. . . .

The Lord considers you a friend. Sin once separated you from God, but Jesus died so that mankind could have **relationship** with the Father.

september

27

relentless

He remembered his covenant with them and **relented** because of his unfailing love.

Psalm 106:45 (NLT)

. . . .

God's mercy is great and His love is **relentless**. He promises to
never give up on you!

relieved

Hear me when I call, O God of my righteousness! You have **relieved** me in my distress; Have mercy on me, and hear my prayer.

Psalm 4:1 (NKJV)

. . . .

Your **relief** in times of distress is found in Jesus. He takes the weight of your burdens upon Himself. Place your worries in His hands!

september

29

religious

Those who consider themselves religious and yet do not keep a tight rein on their tongues deceive themselves, and their **religion** is worthless.

James 1:26 (NIV)

. . . .

As a Christian, you are called to a higher standard than the world. People pay close attention to your actions and words. Christianity isn't just a **religious** term, it is an active pursuit of Jesus.

september

30

remarkable

Ask me and I will tell you **remarkable** secrets you do not know about things to come.

Jeremiah 33:3 (NLT)

. . . .

Ask for and desire insight from the Lord. He wants to reveal His **remarkable** thoughts and plans for you.

october

1

repentant

The sacrifice you desire is a broken spirit. You will not reject a broken and **repentant** heart, O God.

Psalm 51:17 (NLT)

. . . .

Humble yourself before the Lord. Approach Him with a **repentant** heart and He will welcome you with open arms.

october

rescued

He brought me out into a spacious place; he **rescued** me because he delighted in me.

Psalm 18:19 (NIV)

. . . .

Give thanks to the Lord for He is a **Rescuer**! He saves those He loves. He has delivered you from your adversaries.

october

3

reserved

Blessed be the God and Father of our Lord Jesus Christ, who according to His great mercy has caused us to be born again to a living hope through the resurrection of Jesus Christ from the dead, to obtain an inheritance which is imperishable and undefiled and will not fade away, **reserved** in heaven for you . . .

1 Peter 1:3–4 (NASB)

. . . .

The Father has **reserved** a special place in heaven for you. Eternity is ahead. The Lord is great and worthy to be praised!

october

resolved

For I **resolved** to know nothing while I was with you except Jesus Christ and him crucified.

1 Corinthians 2:2 (NIV)

. . . .

Resolve to simply know Jesus Christ. Nothing else in this world truly matters. It is all about Jesus!

october

5

respected

Since we **respected** our earthly fathers who disciplined us, shouldn't we submit even more to the discipline of the Father of our spirits, and live forever?

Hebrews 12:9 (NLT)

. . . .

It is admirable to **respect** men of authority, but esteem the Lord above all else. He is your eternal Father. In Him you have everything.

october

6

responsible

Brothers and sisters, each person, as **responsible** to God, should remain in the situation they were in when God called them.

1 Corinthians 7:24 (NIV)

. . . .

In the end, you are accountable to God alone. Be **responsible** in the tasks to which He has called you!

october

7

rest

By the seventh day God had finished the work he had been doing; so on the seventh day he **rested** from all his work.

Genesis 2:2 (NIV)

. . . .

There is a time to work and a time to be still. Even God rested on the seventh day of creation. Take time to **rest**!

october

8

restored

. . . then that person can pray to God and find favor with him, they will see God's face and shout for joy; he will **restore** them to full well-being.

Job 33:26 (NIV)

. . . .

Cry out to the Lord and He will answer. Give Him the burdens of your past mistakes and the wounds of your heart. You are fully **restored** in Christ.

october

9

revered

"The purpose of my covenant with the Levites was to bring life and peace, and that is what I gave them. This required reverence from them, and they greatly **revered** me and stood in awe of my name."

Malachi 2:5 (NLT)

. . . .

Stand in awe of the Lord. Grant Him the **reverence** of your heart. His intentions are just and right!

october

10

revolutionary

Jesus asked them, "Am I some dangerous **revolutionary**, that you come with swords and clubs to arrest me?"

Matthew 26:55 (NLT)

. . . .

As a follower of Christ, you are called to be **revolutionary**, to bring about radical change in the world. You were not called to just blend in!

october

reward

From the fruit of their lips people are filled with good things, and the work of their hands brings them **reward**.

Proverbs 12:14 (NIV)

. . . .

One of God's promises is that all hard work brings a profit. The Lord **rewards** those who carry out His purposes, and His goodness surrounds them!

october

righteous

The eyes of the LORD are on the **righteous**, and his ears are attentive to their cry . . .

Psalm 34:15 (NIV)

. . . .

You are **righteous** through faith in God's Son. The Father has promised to watch over you, provide for you and answer the cries of your heart. He has set His eyes on you!

october

13

righteousness

Abram believed the LORD, and he credited it to him as **righteousness**.

Genesis 15:6 (NIV)

. . . .

Your heavenly Father loves for you to trust Him. There is no risk because the Lord will never disappoint you. Believe in the Lord and He will credit it to you as **righteousness**, just like He did for Abraham.

october

safe

The name of the LORD is a fortified tower; the righteous run to it and are **safe**.

Proverbs 18:10 (NIV)

. . . .

Do not be afraid. Fear is not of God. The Lord is sovereign, and in Him you are kept **safe**!

october

satisfied

As for me, I will be vindicated and will see your face; when I awake, I will be **satisfied** with seeing your likeness.

Psalm 17:15 (NIV)

. . . .

Always be **satisfied** in the goodness of the Lord. Trust Him in times of trouble and in times of success. He remains constant when everything else fails!

october

16

saved

Heal me, LORD, and I will be healed; **save** me and I will be saved, for you are the one I praise.

Jeremiah 17:14 (NIV)

. . . .

Whatever the Lord does on your behalf can't be undone by another. You're **saved** by His grace, and His power is absolute!

october

savior

But when the kindness and love of God our **Savior** appeared, he saved us, not because of righteous things we had done, but because of his mercy. He saved us through the washing of rebirth and renewal by the Holy Spirit . . .

Titus 3:4–5 (NIV)

. . . .

Jesus Christ is your Redeemer, Restorer, **Savior** and Friend! There is no sin that you cannot lay at His feet in exchange for His righteousness.

october

savor

For we are a sweet **savour** of Christ unto God, in them that are saved, and in them that perish . . .

2 Corinthians 2:15 (KJV)

. . . .

Take time to adore and **savor** the presence of the Lord. Ask Him to fill you with His Spirit so that you will radiate His love even more.

october

19

selected

My friends, you must do all you can to show that God has really chosen and **selected** you. If you keep on doing this, you won't stumble and fall.

2 Peter 1:10 (CEV)

. . . .

You did not accidentally come to Jesus. You were **selected** by God and given a destiny and calling that only you can fulfill!

october

20

selfless

. . . and to put on the new **self**, created to be like God in true righteousness and holiness.

Ephesians 4:24 (NIV)

. . . .

God is righteous, **selfless** and holy. Strive to be more like Him every day. Choose to walk in the newness of life that is yours in Christ.

october

21

sensitive

We who are strong must be considerate of those who are **sensitive** about things like this. We must not just please ourselves. We should help others do what is right and build them up in the Lord.

Romans 15:1–2 (NLT)

. . . .

The Bible says to abstain from things that might cause your brother in Christ to stumble. Be **sensitive** to others by not participating in things that encourage sin. Instead, be an advocate of righteousness.

october

22

sentimental

So this is my prayer: that your love will flourish and that you will not only love much but well. Learn to love appropriately. You need to use your head and test your feelings so that your love is sincere and intelligent, not **sentimental** gush. Live a lover's life, circumspect and exemplary, a life Jesus will be proud of: bountiful in fruits from the soul, making Jesus Christ attractive to all, getting everyone involved in the glory and praise of God.

Philippians 1:9–11 (The Message)

. . . .

Real and unfailing love can only be found in God. Anyone can be **sentimental** and affectionate, but it is the Lord who gives unconditional love. Ask Him to show you how to love others!

october

separated

This includes you who were once far away from God. You were his enemies, **separated** from him by your evil thoughts and actions. Yet now he has reconciled you to himself through the death of Christ in his physical body. As a result, he has brought you into his own presence, and you are holy and blameless as you stand before him without a single fault.

Colossians 1:21–22 (NLT)

. . . .

The sin that once **separated** you from God is no longer an obstacle. He is near! You are the righteousness of Christ, holy and acceptable to the Lord.

october

24

settled

Your people **settled** in it, and from your bounty, God, you provided for the poor.

Psalm 68:10 (NIV)

· ·

The Lord wants to bless you so that you can be a blessing to others. **Settle** yourself in His provision and trust that as you are generous to others, God will be generous to you.

october

25

sharpen

If the axe is dull and he does not **sharpen** its edge, then he must exert more strength. Wisdom has the advantage of giving success.

Ecclesiastes 10:10 (NASB)

. . . .

We're more fruitful and productive when we allow ourselves to be **sharpened** by the Word of God. Day after day, seek the wisdom of the Lord and He will prosper you!

october

26

shine

. . . so that you may become blameless and pure, "children of God without fault in a warped and crooked generation." Then you will **shine** among them like stars in the sky . . .

Philippians 2:15 (NIV)

. . . .

The life that Jesus Christ has placed within you shines brightly to a dark and hurting world. Let your life be a city on a hill. Let your light **shine**!

october

27

significant

Do nothing from selfish ambition or conceit, but in humility count others more **significant** than yourselves.

Philippians 2:3 (ESV)

. . . .

Just as Christ placed your life before His very own, consider the needs of others more **significant** than your own. Let selflessness rule your heart, live to bless others.

october

28

silenced

From the mouth of the righteous comes the fruit of wisdom, but a perverse tongue will be **silenced**.

Proverbs 10:31 (NIV)

. . . .

Your mouth is one of the most powerful tools you possess. Use it to speak positively, and if you can't, simply choose **silence**.

october

29

simplicity

But I fear, lest somehow, as the serpent deceived Eve by his craftiness, so your minds may be corrupted from the **simplicity** that is in Christ.

2 Corinthians 11:3 (NKJV)

. . . .

Faith in Jesus is not complicated or confusing. There are many religions with many doctrines, but nothing compares to the **simplicity** of loving Jesus and trusting Him to do the rest!

october

sincerity

For we are not, as so many, peddling the word of God; but as of **sincerity**, but as from God, we speak in the sight of God in Christ.

2 Corinthians 2:17 (NKJV)

. . . .

Live a life of **sincerity** and authenticity. Be the same person towards all people so that they see Jesus in you!

october

31

skilled

According to the grace of God given to me, like a **skilled** master builder I laid a foundation, and someone else is building upon it. Let each one take care how he builds upon it.

1 Corinthians 3:10 (ESV)

. . . .

You are **skilled** and uniquely gifted for the calling God has placed on your life. Carefully develop the talents you have been given so that you can use them fully for the glory of God!

november

soften

You water all of its fields and level the lumpy ground. You send showers of rain to **soften** the soil and help the plants sprout. Wherever your footsteps touch the earth, a rich harvest is gathered.

Psalm 65:10–11 (CEV)

. . . .

Ask the Lord to **soften** your heart so you can hear Him speak. Let go of your own understanding and knowledge; His ways bring true success!

november

2

solemn

I am going to make a **solemn** promise to you and to everyone who will live after you.

Genesis 9:9 (CEV)

. . . .

All of God's promises are **solemn** and He takes none of them lightly. Trust in the eternal and faithful promises of the Lord!

november

sovereign

The **Sovereign** LORD is my strength; he makes my feet like the feet of a deer, he enables me to tread on the heights.

Habakkuk 3:19 (NIV)

. . . .

What is impossible for man is no challenge for God. He is almighty, full of strength and power. The Lord is **Sovereign** over all the earth!

november

spared

But I have **spared** you for a purpose—to show you my power and to spread my fame throughout the earth.

Exodus 9:16 (NLT)

. . . .

Because you were chosen by God, you've been **spared** from the penalty of sin; therefore, make the name of Jesus famous and share the good news of Salvation with the world!

november

5

special

But you are a chosen people, a royal priesthood, a holy nation, God's **special** possession, that you may declare the praises of him who called you out of darkness into his wonderful light.

1 Peter 2:9 (NIV)

. . . .

The eyes of the Lord watch over you. As a parent takes care of a beloved child, so the Lord cares for you. You are **special**, set apart and irreplaceable to the Father.

november

spectacular

Are we commending ourselves to you again? No, we are giving you a reason to be proud of us, so you can answer those who brag about having a **spectacular** ministry rather than having a sincere heart.

2 Corinthians 5:12 (NLT)

. . . .

Impressive and clever tactics are attractive to the eyes, but a genuine and sincere faith is what counts. It is the love and grace of Jesus that is truly **spectacular**!

november

spiritual

This is what we speak, not in words taught us by human wisdom but in words taught by the Spirit, explaining **spiritual** realities with Spirit-taught words.

1 Corinthians 2:13 (NIV)

. . . .

The Holy Spirit is vital in your understanding of the Word of God. Be continually filled with His Spirit so that your eyes will be opened and your heart will discern **spiritual** things.

november

8

spotless

For you know that God paid a ransom to save you from the empty life you inherited from your ancestors. And the ransom he paid was not mere gold or silver. It was the precious blood of Christ, the sinless, **spotless** Lamb of God.

1 Peter 1:18–19 (NLT)

. . . .

Your inheritance was not purchased with treasures of this world. Jesus paid the price so that you can stand **spotless**, without fault, before the Father in heaven. You owe everything to Him!

november

9

stable

"... it will remain **stable**, like the moon, his throne will endure like the skies."

Psalm 89:37 (NET)

. . . .

Your life is **stable** in the hands of God. You can rest secure in His promises, for His Kingdom stands forever!

november

submitted

For they being ignorant of God's righteousness, and seeking to establish their own righteousness, have not **submitted** to the righteousness of God.

Romans 10:3 (NKJV)

. . . .

You will never obtain righteousness on your own. You efforts are worthless. **Submit** to the Lord and you will inherit the righteousness of Jesus Christ!

november

success

In everything he did he had great **success**, because the LORD was with him.

1 Samuel 18:14 (NIV)

. . . .

True **success** begins and ends with the wisdom of God. Let the Lord direct your steps and He will prosper you!

november

12

successful

Now, my son, the LORD be with you that you may be **successful**, and build the house of the LORD your God just as He has spoken concerning you.

1 Chronicles 22:11 (NASB)

. . . .

Trust in the Lord and you will be **successful** in all that He calls you to do! Man's evaluation of success means nothing; it is God who defines true success.

november

13

sufficient

But he said to me, "My grace is **sufficient** for you, for my power is made perfect in weakness." Therefore I will boast all the more gladly about my weaknesses, so that Christ's power may rest on me.

2 Corinthians 12:9 (NIV)

. . . .

The Lord is more than **sufficient** for you. Your weaknesses are only opportunities for God's power to manifest. When you are weak, He is strong!

november

14

supported

You have given me the shield of your salvation, and your right hand **supported** me, and your gentleness made me great.

Psalm 18:35 (ESV)

. . . .

When you fall, hold on to Jesus! He will pick you up and **support** you with His mighty hand. You are not alone.

november

15

surpassed

"This is the one I meant when I said, 'A man who comes after me has **surpassed** me because he was before me.'"

John 1:30 (NIV)

. . . .

The perfection of Jesus **surpassed** all men. There has never been and never will be another as awesome as He. He is altogether beautiful!

november

16

surrender

And if I give all my possessions to feed the poor, and if I **surrender** my body to be burned, but do not have love, it profits me nothing.

1 Corinthians 13:3 (NASB)

. . . .

You can **surrender** everything to this world, but if you do not show people the love of Christ, then your sacrifice is of no value. God's love will set you apart!

november

sustenance

If your instructions hadn't **sustained** me with joy, I would have died in my misery.

Psalm 119:92 (NLT)

. . . .

If you do not give your body regular **sustenance**, you cannot thrive physically. In this same way, if you do not feed your spirit the Word of God, you will become spiritually unhealthy.

sweetness

Pleasant words are like a honeycomb, **sweetness** to the soul and health to the bones.

Proverbs 16:24 (NKJV)

. . . .

Words hold the power of life and death. Use your mouth to inspire and praise so that others will know the **sweetness** of Christ.

sympathetic

Finally, all of you, be like-minded, be **sympathetic**, love one another, be compassionate and humble.

1 Peter 3:8 (NIV)

. . . .

Your Father in heaven has great compassion for you and He weeps when you weep. In this same way, be **sympathetic** towards others and help carry the burdens of their sorrow.

november

20

talent

As each of you has received a gift (a particular spiritual **talent**, a gracious divine endowment), employ it for one another as [befits] good trustees of God's many-sided grace [faithful stewards of the extremely diverse powers and gifts granted to Christians by unmerited favor].

1 Peter 4:10 (AMP)

. . . .

You have been given many **talents** by God Himself for the glory of His name. Surrender your gifts and abilities to His purposes and He will give you favor and success!

tamed

For every kind of beast and bird, of reptile and sea creature, can be **tamed** and has been tamed by mankind, but no human being can tame the tongue. It is a restless evil, full of deadly poison.

James 3:7–8 (ESV)

. . . .

On your own, you cannot **tame** your tongue. Avoid gossip at all costs. Give the Lord complete control of your tongue and He will help you speak words of life!

november

22

tenderness

Therefore if you have any encouragement from being united with Christ, if any comfort from his love, if any common sharing in the Spirit, if any **tenderness** and compassion, then make my joy complete by being like-minded, having the same love, being one in spirit and of one mind.

Philippians 2:1–2 (NIV)

. . . .

The Lord longs for His children to be of one heart and mind, not disputing over useless matters. With **tender** hearts, as one body, share in the goodness and love of Christ!

november

thankful

Let the peace of Christ rule in your hearts, since as members of one body you were called to peace. And be **thankful**.

Colossians 3:15 (NIV)

. . . .

Always be **thankful** for the gift of life. Live at peace with others and do not take any single day for granted. Life is precious!

november

24

thirst

"... but whoever drinks the water I give them will never **thirst**.
Indeed, the water I give them will become in them a spring of
water welling up to eternal life."

John 4:14 (NIV)

. . . .

Jesus is the Living Water. He satisfies your **thirst** with His life.
He is the Well that never runs dry!

november

25

thoughtful

Isn't it obvious that conspirators lose out, while the **thoughtful** win love and trust?

Proverbs 14:22 (The Message)

. . . .

The Lord is attentive to the needs of His children. He is **thoughtful**, kind, generous and merciful. He is worthy of all your love and trust.

timeless

There is a **time** for everything, and a season for every activity under the heavens . . .

Ecclesiastes 3:1 (NIV)

. . . .

Life has seasons of plenty and seasons of lack. Everything under the sun is subject to change, but the statutes of the Lord are **timeless**.

november

27

trained

No discipline seems pleasant at the time, but painful. Later on, however, it produces a harvest of righteousness and peace for those who have been **trained** by it.

Hebrews 12:11 (NIV)

. . . .

The Lord has equipped and **trained** you for life. He has given you His Word and all of His precious promises so that you might walk in righteousness and peace.

transparent

The twelve gates were twelve pearls, each gate made of a single pearl. The great street of the city was of gold, as pure as **transparent** glass.

Revelation 21:21 (NIV)

· ·

Just as you have the ability to see through glass, the Lord sees through your actions straight to your heart. Live a life of **transparency** so that your motives are never questioned.

treasured

Your word I have **treasured** in my heart, That I may not sin against You.

Psalm 119:11 (NASB)

. . . .

Treasure God's Word in your heart. It will guide and protect you. His Word will lead you to righteousness and peace.

november

30

triumph

I trust in you; do not let me be put to shame, nor let my enemies **triumph** over me.

Psalm 25:2 (NIV)

. . . .

There is no shame in trusting the Lord. Darkness has no hope. God is **triumphant**!

december

trust

Trust in the Lord with all your heart and lean not on your own understanding; in all your ways submit to him, and he will make your paths straight.

Proverbs 3:5–6 (NIV)

. . . .

It brings great joy to the Father's heart when you **trust** Him. He can see far beyond what your human eyes can see. Let Him order your steps and make your way clear.

trustworthy

The law of the LORD is perfect, refreshing the soul. The statutes of the LORD are **trustworthy**, making wise the simple.

Psalm 19:7 (NIV)

. . . .

Everything pertaining to the Lord is **trustworthy**. His ways are far above your ways and His thoughts higher than your thoughts. He is altogether perfect!

december

truth

Truthful words stand the test of time, but lies are soon exposed.

Proverbs 12:19 (NLT)

. . . .

Anytime light and darkness meet, light always wins. It is the same with **truth** and lies. Truth always wins and lasts forever!

december

4

unconditional

Pay attention and come to me! Listen, so you can live! Then I will make an **unconditional** covenantal promise to you, just like the reliable covenantal promises I made to David.

Isaiah 55:3 (NET)

. . . .

If a promise is **unconditional**, there is nothing you can or can't do that will nullify that promise. When you accepted Jesus as your Savior, His grace flooded your life—and there is nothing you can or can't do that will break His covenant!

december

undefeated

. . . but we can win with God's help. He will **defeat** our enemies.

Psalm 108:13 (NCV)

. . . .

You can walk **undefeated** and victorious over every enemy that comes against you. The Lord arms you with strength for battle and gives you the power to break the chains of sin!

december

6

understood

This same Good News that came to you is going out all over the world. It is bearing fruit everywhere by changing lives, just as it changed your lives from the day you first heard and **understood** the truth about God's wonderful grace.

Colossians 1:6 (NLT)

. . . .

Whenever the power of God's magnificent grace is **understood**, change happens! God's grace is the strength you need to overcome every ounce of sin in your life.

december

undeserved

"We believe that we are all saved the same way, by the **undeserved** grace of the Lord Jesus."

Acts 15:11 (NLT)

. . . .

The grace you have received, through the death of God's Son on the cross, is completely **undeserved**. His amazing grace is a gift, the most beautiful and costly gift that has ever been given.

december

unlimited

I pray that from his glorious, **unlimited** resources he will empower you with inner strength through his Spirit.

Ephesians 3:16 (NLT)

. . . .

Think about this: The resources of the Lord are **unlimited**. The entirety of the universe belongs to His care, and all power, authority and strength is His! He holds all that you need.

untainted

No lie was found to be upon their lips, for they are blameless (spotless, **untainted**, without blemish) before the throne of God.

Revelation 14:5 (AMP)

. . . .

The righteousness of Jesus will present you **untainted** before the Father. You will be white as snow. Your lips will shamelessly and eternally praise Him!

december

10

upheld

His heart is **upheld**, he will not fear, until he looks with satisfaction on his adversaries.

Psalm 112:8 (NASB)

. . . .

The Lord will never leave you alone in trouble. He promises to **uphold** you with His mighty hand. Victory is inevitable when God is by your side!

december

11

uplifted

For You are the glory of their strength [their proud adornment], and by Your favor our horn is exalted and we walk with **uplifted** faces!

Psalm 89:17 (AMP)

. . . .

Let the joy of the Lord be in your heart and on your face so that you might be **uplifting** to others when they see you. A smile can encourage and bless someone just as much as words.

december

12

upright

The sacrifice of the wicked is an abomination to the LORD, but the prayer of the **upright** is His delight.

Proverbs 15:8 (NKJV)

. . . .

Walk out your faith in a manner that is **upright**, pertaining to the ways of the Lord. This brings great delight to your Father in heaven.

december

13

valor

And the angel of the LORD appeared to him and said to him, "The LORD is with you, O mighty man of **valour**."

Judges 6:12 (ESV)

. . . .

Walk in confidence, bravery and **valor** for the King of Kings, the Great I Am is with you. He knows no fear or defeat!

december

value

The refining pot is for silver and the furnace for gold, and a man is **valued** by what others say of him.

Proverbs 27:21 (NKJV)

. . . .

Ultimately, your **value** is not determined by man, but always walk in integrity so that others speak good things of you. You are called to be like Christ, to love others with the love He has lavished on you.

december

15

vastness

How precious to me are your thoughts, God! How **vast** is the sum of them!

Psalm 139:17 (NIV)

. . . .

Not a moment goes by when your heavenly Father is not thinking of you. His thoughts are **vast** and innumerable, full of love and adoration.

december

victory

Don't be afraid, for I am with you. Don't be discouraged, for I am your God. I will strengthen you and help you. I will hold you up with my **victorious** right hand.

Isaiah 41:10 (NLT)

. . . .

The Lord does not promise that the battles you face will be easily won, but He does promise **victory**! In the times you feel defeated, proclaim the name of the Lord over your circumstances.

december

17

virtue

For the righteous LORD loves justice. The **virtuous** will see his face.

Psalm 11:7 (NLT)

. . . .

Always seek to live **virtuously** so that others might see your way of life and be drawn to Jesus. The Lord's face will shine upon you and His favor will be on all you do.

december

warm

If you say to that person, "God be with you! I hope you stay **warm** and get plenty to eat," but you do not give what that person needs, your words are worth nothing.

James 2:16 (NCV)

. . . .

With a **warm** and loving heart, meet the needs of the broken and poor. Live out the love, grace, provision and goodness that Jesus has shown you.

december

welcome

Therefore, my brothers and sisters, make every effort to confirm your calling and election. For if you do these things, you will never stumble, and you will receive a rich **welcome** into the eternal kingdom of our Lord and Savior Jesus Christ.

2 Peter 1:10–11 (NIV)

Even when you're in the midst of sin, your Father in heaven **welcomes** you with open arms. Run to Him, you are forgiven and loved.

wholehearted

Dear brothers and sisters, honor those who are your leaders in the Lord's work. They work hard among you and give you spiritual guidance. Show them great respect and **wholehearted** love because of their work. And live peacefully with each other.

1 Thessalonians 5:12–13 (NLT)

Whatever you do, be **wholehearted** in your efforts. Do everything as though for the Lord Himself to bring Him glory and honor!

whole

He is the atoning sacrifice for our sins, and not only for ours but also for the sins of the **whole** world.

1 John 2:2 (NIV)

. . . .

Jesus did not die for the sins of part of the world; He died for the sins of the **whole** world. There is not one person on this earth who cannot come to Jesus and be set free.

december

wisdom

I keep asking that the God of our Lord Jesus Christ, the glorious Father, may give you the Spirit of **wisdom** and revelation, so that you may know him better.

Ephesians 1:17 (NIV)

. . . .

The **wisdom** that comes from God is full of favor, success and prosperity. A heart that seeks God's wisdom will begin to know the inexhaustible depths of His knowledge, understanding and power.

december

23

winner

An unlucky loser is shunned by all, but everyone loves a **winner**.

Proverbs 14:20 (The Message)

. . . .

In Christ, you have **won** already. You have passed the test and overcome defeat. Celebrate the victorious life you have in Jesus!

december

24

wonder

"I see that the Lord is always with me. I will not be shaken, for he is right beside me. No **wonder** my heart is glad, and my tongue shouts his praises! My body rests in hope."

Acts 2:25–26 (NLT)

. . . .

Stand in **wonder** and amazement of the goodness of the Lord! He blesses you in ways you cannot even begin to understand. In Him there is always hope!

december

25

wonderfully

I praise you because I am fearfully and **wonderfully** made;
your works are wonderful, I know that full well.

Psalm 139:14 (NIV)

. . . .

You were created, designed and destined by the God of the
universe. He knows every hair on your head and every breath
you will take. You are uniquely and **wonderfully** made!

december

worship

Jesus answered, "It is written: '**Worship** the Lord your God and serve him only.'"

Luke 4:8 (NIV)

. . . .

Worship God with your whole life. There is no other thing or being that deserves your praise. The Lord stands alone!

december

27

worthiness

Great is the LORD! He is most **worthy** of praise! No one can measure his greatness.

Psalm 145:3 (NLT)

. . . .

The Lord has proven His **worthiness**! He deserves all of your glory, honor, praise and devotion. There is no one more worthy in all the earth.

december

yearning

I long and **yearn** for the courts of the LORD; my heart and flesh cry out for the living God.

Psalm 84:2 (HCSB)

. . . .

Cry out to the Lord and let Him satisfy the **yearning** in your heart. Above all else, desire to be in His presence.

december

yes

For no matter how many promises God has made, they are "**Yes**" in Christ. And so through him the "Amen" is spoken by us to the glory of God.

2 Corinthians 1:20 (NIV)

. . . .

Your heavenly Father says "**yes**" to you! Just as an earthly father wants to bless his children, God wants to bless you. Trust Him with the dreams and desires in your heart!

youthfulness

Even **youths** grow tired and weary, and young men stumble and fall; but those who hope in the LORD will renew their strength. They will soar on wings like eagles; they will run and not grow weary, they will walk and not be faint.

Isaiah 40:30–31 (NIV)

. . . .

The vitality and energy of **youthfulness** is fleeting. But remember, no matter what age you are, the Lord wants to renew your strength, give you new hope and new enthusiasm for life!

december

31

zeal

. . . looking for the blessed hope and glorious appearing of our great God and Savior Jesus Christ, who gave Himself for us, that He might redeem us from every lawless deed and purify for Himself His own special people, **zealous** for good works.

Titus 2:13–14 (NKJV)

. . . .

Focus your **zeal** towards the purposes of God! You will see incredible blessing and prosperity.